Zorica Herbst-Krausz

OLD JEWISH DISHES

Corvina

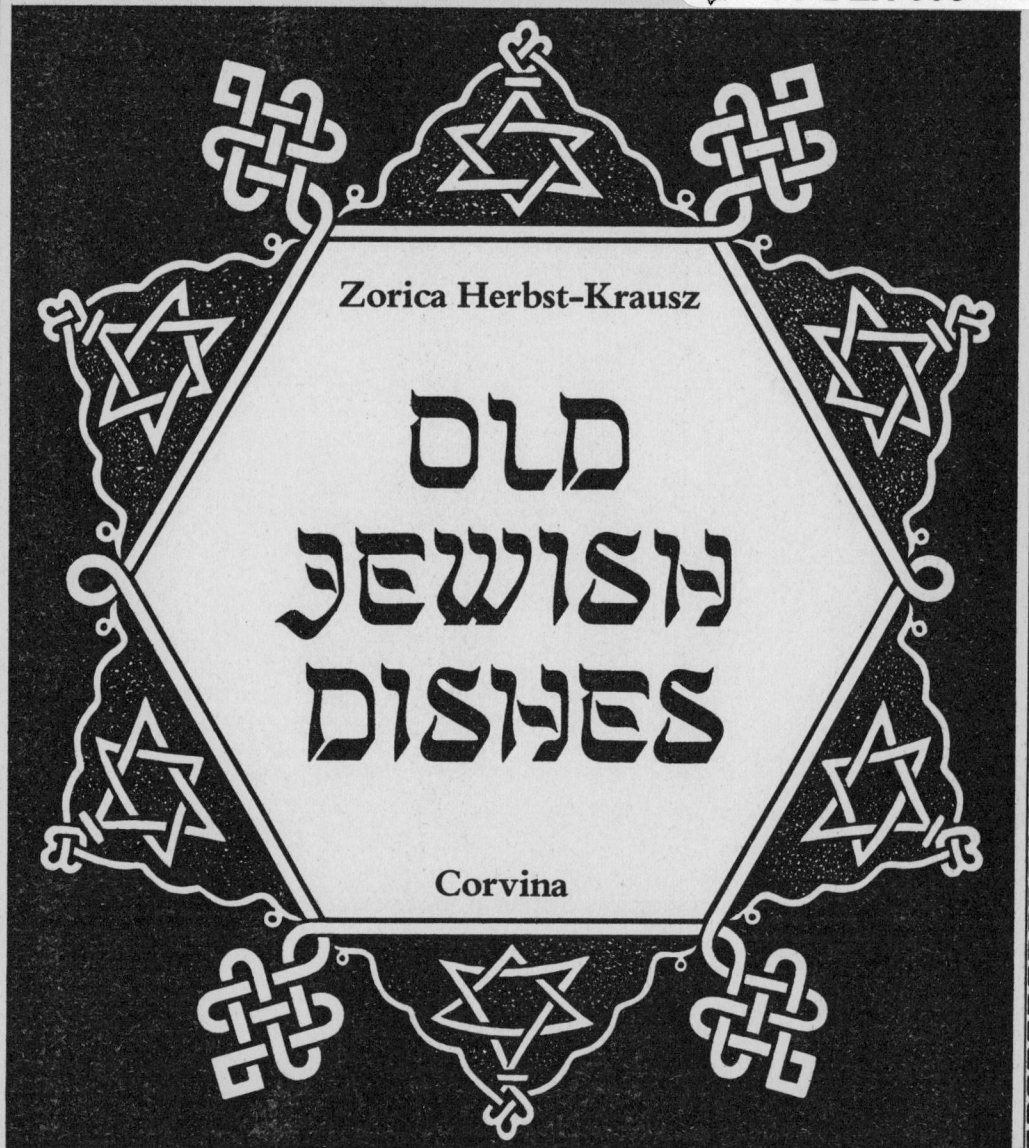

Title of the Hungarian original: *Régi zsidó ételek,*
Corvina, Budapest, 1988

Introduction by Dr József Schweitzer,
Director of the National Institute of Rabbinical Studies
Consultants for the English edition:
J. Audrey Ellison and Josephine Bacon

Translated by Maria Sail

Colour photographs by András Szebeni

Dishes prepared by István Lukács, Executive Chef of the Atrium Hyatt Hotel, Budapest
Pastries prepared by Péter N. Gombai, Head Patissier of the Atrium Hyatt Hotel, Budapest

© Zorica Herbst-Krausz
ISBN 963 13 2529 6

TABLE OF CONTENTS

Introduction 4

Preface 5

The Jewish Calendar 6

The Sabbath 7
Festivals of Pilgrimage 9
Days of Atonement 12
Festivals of Joy 14
Festivals of Mourning 15
Family Celebrations 15

Ritual Prescriptions 19

Foods of Vegetable Origin 21
Bread and Challah (Barhes) 21

Recipes 23

Soups 24
Soup Garnishes 30
Sauces 33
Accompaniments 35
Vegetables 38
Fish 42
Meat Dishes 47
Perishable Stuffings 55
Tasty Tidbits 57
Kugels and Noodles 59
Pastries 60

Table of Recipes 73

INTRODUCTION

The author of this volume not only presents a collection of specialities of Jewish cuisine—which, alone, would be an interesting and worthwhile task—she goes further and presents a survey of the most important of the Hungarian-Jewish traditions. Thus, in addition to delightful dishes, the reader will be able to sample Jewish culture and civilisation. A few of the characteristics of Jewish culinary tradition dating from the days of the Torah and the Talmud will be presented, although by no means a complete collection.

The Torah calls a meal among family and guests *mishte,* from the Hebrew word for 'drink', so we can assume that the meal was accompanied by drinks, probably wine. Another kind of meal eaten by the family or guests was called *zevah mishpaha;* these were arranged to celebrate the New Moon, and other festivals, as well as family events such as weaning or marriage. From the Torah we learn of the lavish entertainments of the Egyptian Pharaoh, the Persian King Ahasuerus and his Jewish wife, Queen Esther, and many others.

Talmudic literature contains much advice about hygiene and eating habits. In general, one is urged to eat with moderation, and not to serve a succession of sumptuous courses, especially as it was considered as unhealthy to eat too much as it was to eat too fast. We also know that the diet of the nobility in Talmudic times included fresh vegetables, salads, radishes and the like, showing that the attitude to diet was very enlightened.

Fish has been popular in Jewish cooking since the captivity in Egypt; it is a symbol of plenty and fertility. The braided Sabbath bread is also an important ethnographic symbol. In Hungary, it is called *barhes* from the German word *Bercht* = braid; it is known as *challah* (hala) in Hebrew.

Jewish ethics stresses the importance of intellectual pleasures along with the pleasures of dining. If there are three people at a festive table and there is no interpretation of the Divine Word, the meal is as gloomy as a burial feast. Interpretation and discussion of Talmudic literature is an ancient and beautiful form of Jewish dining-room conversation, but one reserved for the Sabbath. On weekdays, there are no opportunities for such discussions, but on Saturdays one should make up for it, especially at the third meal of the day of rest, the *Se'udah Shelishit,* eaten before nightfall on Saturday. Teaching, singing and prayer make these hours beautiful and unforgettable.

The recipes contained in this book preserve the Jewish culinary customs of Central Europe—and especially Hungary—at a time when, four decades after the Holocaust, this type of gastronomy is practised by only a very few. In my opinion this gives the work an added value.

Dr József Schweitzer

PREFACE

When I started my research in the second half of the 1970s, I found very few books in library catalogues that dealt with the preparation of the various Hungarian-Jewish dishes. There are two noteworthy exceptions: Mrs Márton Rosenfeld's *A zsidónő szakácskönyve* (Jewish Woman's Cookery Book) and the book by Mrs Gitti Rand Adler (Aunt Gitti) entitled *A zsidó háziasszony könyve* (The Jewish Housewife's Book). These books adapted European culinary arts to the ritual requirements of Jewish cooking. Thanks to these books, valuable dishes were preserved which would otherwise have been lost. I also had the opportunity of reading Margit Löb's book which was published abroad and I used information from her book as well. The works of Ede Vadász, published in various places, were also extremely useful. While reading these sources, I decided that in view of the available data I would restrict my work to cover the period from the turn of the century until today.

I devised a plan for collection and description of recipes but this plan would have remained in its initial stages if not for the help of Dr Tibor Bodrogi, the recently deceased director of the Ethnographic Research Group of the Hungarian Academy of Sciences, Dr Márton Istvánovics, the group leader, and Zsuzsa Erdélyi, who has been my mentor and patron since the inception of the work. I have tried through this book to express my gratitude and be worthy of their trust and good will.

I was able to start the research and collection of material with the help of Hermann Fixler, President of the Orthodox Jewish Religious Community of Budapest. At this point, I would like to express my gratitude to all those who patiently helped me along and gave their very best. I would like to mention especially Mrs Zsigmond Holzer and Sara Salamon (who has since died), from whom I received the greatest assistance.

My work records the practical aspects of Jewish everyday life. I hope that I have managed to preserve and maintain the spiritual traditions learned from my parents, as the keeping of ritual laws are the mainstay of one's religious affiliation.

Zorica Herbst-Krausz

THE JEWISH CALENDAR

Jewish women are bound by strict ritual laws governing the conduct of their household activities. These prohibitions have been handed down from generation to generation. Housewives need great ingenuity to prepare a variety of dishes while adhering to these restrictions. Tradition has also played an important role in the evolution of Jewish culinary culture.

First of all, the ritual laws should be explained, so that we may be able to better understand the rules governing diet. One of the most important components of this is the calendar, the *luah*, which is drawn up each year according to well-defined rules.

The Jewish calendar, like those of several peoples in the Middle East, is based on the lunar cycle, and the first day of the New Moon is celebrated. The computation of time—according to a theoretical work—starts with the Creation of the World; from that day to 1988, 5748 years are supposed to have elapsed. In leap years, the 12 lunar months are supplemented with a thirteenth month. The first day of the New Year comes a few months before that in the Gregorian calendar. The following are the names of the Jewish months (the corresponding months in the Gregorian calendar are shown in parentheses): *Tishri* (September-October); *Heshan* or *Marheshan* (October-November); *Kislev* (November-December); *Tevet* (December-January); *Shevat* (January-February); *Adar* (February-March); *Nisan* (March-April); *Iyyar* (April-May); *Sivan* (May-June); *Tammuz* (June-July); *Av* or *Menahem Av* (July-August); *Elul* (August-September); in leap years, after the month of Adar comes *Adar Sheni,* in other words, the Second Adar. In the Jewish calendar, the leap year falls only every eleventh year. Jewish festivals influence cooking and eating habits and the preparation of food. The most frequent festival is the Sabbath, in Hebrew *shabbat* (*shabbes* in Yiddish).

The Jewish festivals include three week-long holidays which were once occasions for pilgrimage—Passover *(Pesah),* Pentecost *(Shavuot)* and Tabernacles *(Succot).* There are two major days of repentance for sins, the New Year *(Rosh Hashana)* and the Day of Atonement *(Yom Kippur).*

Besides the main festivals, the Jewish calendar includes half-holidays, historical memorial days, and celebrations such as the Day of the Rededication of the Temple in Jerusalem, *Hanukkah,* also known as the Festival of Light, and the Biblical *Purim* or Feast of Lots, the origin of which can be found in the Book of Esther.

Besides the Day of Atonement, there are other days of fasting in the Jewish calendar, mainly days of mourning. These include *Tish'a be-Av (Tishebov* in Yiddish), the ninth day of the month of Av, commemorating the destruction of the First and Second Temples in Jerusalem.

The festivals, half-holidays, days commemorating historical events, and days of mourning are as follows:

Passover 15–22 Nisan (March-April)
Shavuot 6–7 Sivan (May-June)
Succot 15–22 Tishri (September-October)
New Year 1–2 Tishri (September-October)
Yom Kippur 10 Tishri (September-October)
Hanukkah 25 Kislev (November-December) to 2 Tevet (December-January)
Purim 14 Adar (February-March)
Tish'a be-Av 9 Av (July-August).

The length of the festivals is not identical, there are one-day and two-day festivals and there are those that last for several days; in the week-long festivals, the intermediate days between the first two days and the last day are considered as half-holidays.

Family events play an important role in the life of Jewish families: the birth of a male child and his acceptance into the covenant of Abraham by circumcision, then, at thirteen, his initiation into manhood to become a fully-fledged member of the Jewish community *(Bar Mitzvah),* as well as betrothals, weddings and funerals.

The Sabbath

Saturday—the Sabbath—is the day of rest. From Friday evening until Saturday evening, time is devoted to complete spiritual and physical rest. The Sabbath involves abstinence from cooking and the prohibition on lighting a fire. The purpose of this festival is to remind us of the Creation and the Creator, who rested on the seventh day. The oldest description of the Sabbath is found in the Torah, the Five Books of Moses. In accordance with the Bible, all the world celebrates one day of the week as a day of rest.

This rest, however, requires a lot of preparatory work by the housewife. All the Saturday meals have to be cooked ahead of time and because it is forbidden to light a fire, the cooked food has to be kept hot in an oven lit on Friday before dusk.

In former times, *cholent,* the Sabbath stew, was taken to the bakery on Friday so that it could be served piping hot at Saturday noon. One may not cook for more than one day ahead, except on festivals lasting for several days, or on a festival day which immediately precedes the Sabbath. On those occasions—after performing the ceremony called *Eruv Tanshilin*—one was allowed to cook food for the following day.

According to the ancients, Jewish people are endowed with a second soul on Saturdays (*neshama yetera* in Hebrew, *nehsumeh yesereh* in Yiddish) and therefore they are able to consume with a better appetite the delicacies served to them.

The housewife has to budget her time wisely; the house has to be sparkling clean, the holiday clothes have to be laid out for all the members of the family, the candlesticks must be brightly polished, the *barhes (challah)* has to be ready to greet the holy day covered by an embroidered cloth.

It is the housewife's duty to light and bless the candles before the Sabbath. After the start of the Sabbath, the husband and male children come home from the synagogue and receive the blessing. Then they sit around a table which is covered with the best white tablecloth.

On the Sabbath and every festival except fast days and Passover, the bread Jews eat is *barhes,* which is made from a richer dough than ordinary bread. The preparation of this bread begins on Thursday, when the yeast starter is prepared; the bread is kneaded, braided and baked on Friday morning according to specific rules. For instance, the housewife must take a small piece of dough the size of an egg and throw it in the fire, while reciting a prayer. Today, this is done in Jewish bakeries under the supervision of the *mashgiah,* the religious supervisor. This ceremony is performed in memory of the flour offerings in the Temple. Thereafter, the dough is braided, or braided and coiled, and sprinkled with poppy seed. Besides the *barhes,* a breakfast yeast bread and a coffee cake filled with cottage cheese *(delkli)* are frequently served in Hungary. An egg-pie *(eierkihli)* is eaten after the Saturday morning blessing over the bread. On Thursday or Friday morning, the housewife takes the fowl—goose, duck or chicken—to be served on Friday evening, to the *shohet,* the ritual slaughterer. When he has slaughtered the meat, the *shohet* examines it for any discoloration under the feathers. The down feathers are removed by singeing, carefully turning the fowl over a flame. After the outside is cleaned, the animal is cut open and the insides are carefully examined for signs of disease or damage, which would preclude the consumption of the animal. Only after these procedures is it permitted to cut up the fowl and to kosher the various parts.

Friday evening is associated with *gefillte fish* (stuffed fish), a sort of hors-d'œuvre served before the golden chicken soup; then there is a roast with egg-barley and finally cakes and fruit compote. Where fish is not liked, a so-called *mock fish* is prepared. In olden times, Hungarian Jews prepared corn-on-the-cob for the long evenings ahead and snacked on it during conversation.

Saturday breakfast consists of *barhes* or *delkli* with milk or coffee. On Saturday morning, cold jellied gefillte fish may be eaten. For the midday meal, the *cholent,* a stew slow-cooked overnight, is served; in the summertime, French (green) beans or cold courgettes (zucchini) are also put on the table. In the afternoon, a small snack may be taken after the customary walk. The third meal of the day, the *Se'udah Shelishit,* is also served in the afternoon at home, but for the men it is sometimes eaten at the synagogue. Leavetaking of the Sabbath is celebrated with the ceremony of the *havdala,* the separation between holy day, the Sabbath, and weekday. This is considered a sad ceremony, and it is delayed as long as possible so that the Sabbath should last longer.

The *havdala* ceremony consists of lighting a plaited candle which has several wicks, the inhaling of aromatic spices, and the recitation of a special blessing. Finally, the candle is doused in wine or milk; this signifies taking leave of the Sabbath. Jews wish each other a good week, look back on the Sabbath holiday and look fondly forward to its return the following week. The celebrants wish each other *shavua tov*, 'Good week'.

Festivals of Pilgrimage

Pesah

Festivals of pilgrimage date back to the days of the Temple in Jerusalem; in those days, it was everyone's sacred duty to take an offering to Jerusalem and present it in the Temple. Those who did not make the pilgrimage celebrated it at home. *Passover* is the first festival of pilgrimage, in the order in which they are mentioned in the Bible. Passover commemorates the Exodus from Egypt. The word Passover (*Pesah,* in Hebrew) means that the Angel of Death smote the Egyptians but passed over the houses of the Jews, who were able to start their journey into the desert from captivity towards freedom.

This festival was celebrated in its most ancient form on the fourteenth day of Nisan with a roasted lamb, unleavened bread, bitter herbs and salads. From this evolved the ceremony of the *Seder*, the Passover meal. This festival lasts for eight days. The ancient customs have changed much over the years, but the essence of the festival has remained the same.

Passover requires the greatest and most elaborate preparation of all the festivals. All fermentable foodstuffs (leaven) have to be removed from the house; these foods are called *hametz*. The dishes and utensils used all year round are replaced by dishes used only for Passover. The house has to be thoroughly cleaned, all crumbs of *hametz* have to be removed. During Passover, Jews eat very different foods from their normal diet; instead of bread, they eat *matzo,* also called *pasca* in Hungary, the unleavened bread. At this time, pickled beets, prepared after *Purim,* about a month earlier, are served, from which a tasty sour soup is made. The main item of the diet has become the potato, as it is forbidden to Ashkenazi Jews to eat beans, peas and lentils. Potato flour (*farina)* is an important cooking ingredient, and another essential ingredient is *matzo* in its various forms, such as *matzo* meal, ground fine, medium and coarse. *Matzo* is made of flour and water. The origin of the flour is of the utmost importance. At the time of sowing, orthodox Jews leave a separate row of wheat for just this purpose, and this wheat is harvested with special care. The wheat is called *shemura* (guarded) wheat. Storing and grinding this wheat requires special attention; the flour sacks are kept in a dry place to avoid the formation of mould. Grinding is supervised by a rabbi. This flour is used solely for making *matzos,* the preparation of which was and still is a communal activity. It is a great honour to be asked to perform this task. Even today, all the work involved is carefully divided among the male community members. When preparing *matzos,* there can be no foreign substance even in the vicinity, the bowl and work surface have to be spotless. The person doing the kneading needs a lot of water, as he has to wash his hands often. The kneaded dough is beaten with steel rolling pins. No more than 17 minutes must elapse between kneading and baking. Today, most *matzos* are factory made, under the supervision of the *mashgiah*.

Preparation for the festival is not over yet. There still remains the acquisition of the Passover wine. Wine is made from grapes in tubs set aside for this purpose and is stored in special barrels. Bottling is done with care. The bottles are labelled *Shel Pesah* (for Passover). The bottles are sealed and a rabbi adds his insignia with the *hehsher* (certificate of *kashrus*).

The ingredients of the Seder plate must be prepared. This plate is placed on the dining table and contains a roasted egg, horseradish, a lamb shank bone, celery and a paste mixture of apples, cinnamon, nuts and wine called *haroset*. The first and second evening meals of the festival are called the *Seder,* meaning 'order', which in this case means that whatever is eaten, whatever is drunk, and whatever is said follows a set order. The table is covered with the best tablecloth and the symbolic dishes are placed on this table: the Seder plate, *matzo,* cups of wine and special embroidered cover for the *matzo,* in which three unbroken *matzo* are placed.

In the middle of the Seder plate is the *maror,* a bitter herb, in most cases horseradish, symbolizing the bitterness of life in Egypt. The shank bone of a lamb is placed to the right of it; it is not eaten. This is in memory of the sacrificial lamb of Passover, offered in the Temple.

To the left of the bone is the roasted egg, symbolizing the life cycle and the rebirth of nature in spring. Originally, it was served in memory of the sacrifices offered in the Temple. On the right of the bone is the *haroset,* the mixture symbolizing the mortar used by the Hebrews in their Egyptian captivity. Below, on the left, is the *carpas,* which may consist of celery, parsley or lettuce but it can also be boiled potatoes. This symbolizes the renewal of nature; in the path of newly-grown greenery there is the hope of salvation.

Next to the Seder plate a small dish is placed containing salt water, symbolizing the tears of the Hebrew slaves. The *carpas* is dipped into this bowl during the Seder, and hard-boiled eggs are eaten with the salt water just before the meal. The leader of the Seder, most often the head of the family, serves the symbolic dishes to the participants, with the exception of the shank bone and the roasted egg, which may only be looked at. A further requisite of the Seder table is the wine. During the course of the evening, all participants have to drink four glasses of wine, as the story of the Exodus is told four times in the Book of Exodus. A fifth cup is set aside and reserved for the Prophet Elijah. The door is left ajar, and at the end of the evening it is opened wide, so that the prophet may enter. A special armchair is also set aside for him.

The Seder service is laid down exactly in the special prayerbook called the *Haggadah*. At communal Seders, the most influential member of the community leads the service, but wherever the Seder is held, it is always the youngest person present who asks the 'four questions'. It is traditional for other participants to be allocated portions to read from their copies of the Haggadah. The foods laid out symbolically on the Seder plate are consumed according to ritual at the appropriate times. After dinner, there is singing, playing of games, and riddles are posed to the children to keep them awake. The final ritual of the Seder is the search for the *afikomen,* a piece of *matzo* which is hidden during the meal. This is an exciting pastime for the children as the finder gets a reward.

Shavuot

The second festival of pilgrimage is *Shavuot* (*Shavuos* in Yiddish), the Feast of Weeks. Originally, it was a harvest festival, but it later acquired religious connotations. On this day, God revealed the Torah (the Pentateuch) to his people. The main purpose of the festival, the presentation of the first crops in the Temple, survived, so that at these times the synagogue and Jewish homes are decorated with branches and flowers. At religious services, the Book of Ruth is read from the Bible, describing agricultural life and ancient peasant customs. The festival is so called because seven weeks are counted from the second day of Passover to Shavuot. This is the so-called Counting of the Omer, in memory of the first barley offering of which one portion equalled one *omer* (about 6⅕ imperial pints or one American gallon) of threshed barley.

The period of the Counting of the Omer *(sefirat ha-Omer)* is one of sadness and mourning because the worst troubles seem to have beset the Jews at this time of the year. There were Jewish persecutions in 135 B.C.E., during the reign of Hadrian, as well as in the Middle Ages, in 1096 C.E. and during the Crusades; in 1944, in Hungary, the deportation of the Jews commenced. At this time, all gaiety is forbidden in Jewish homes, with the exception of the 33rd day of the *Omer,* the *Lag ba'Omer*. On this day, the pestilence, which devastated the martyrs, the followers of Rabbi Akiba, who were fighting a war of liberation against the Romans, came to an end. It is the only day during the Counting of the Omer when marriages may be performed.

Thus the Counting of the Omer is a link between the two festivals of pilgrimage, Passover and Shavuot.

Since the Shavuot psalms compare the Torah with milk and honey, it is customary to consume dishes prepared with milk during the festival.

Succot

The third festival of pilgrimage is *Succot* (*Sukkes* in Yiddish), the Feast of Tabernacles. Originally, it was a wheat and grape harvest festival. Later it commemorated the wanderings of the Jews in the desert. The tabernacles remind us of their original significance, as the population who took part in the grape harvest lived in booths or temporary dwellings. The symbol of the tabernacle remained, but its meaning changed significantly. The seventh day of Succot is also the festival of *Hoshana Rabba,* the Great Hosannah; the eighth day is also the festival of *Shemini Atzeret,* the Eighth Day of Solemn Assembly. This is followed immediately by the one-day festival of *Simhat Torah (Simches Toireh* in Yiddish), the Rejoicing of the Law. This joyous holiday is just as rich in symbolism as is Passover. It celebrates the ending of the cycle of reading from the Torah, the Five Books of Moses, and the beginning of a new cycle.

For the Feast of Tabernacles, Jews construct booths with wooden walls, and roofs partly open to the sky, so that the stars can shine in. The insides of the booths are decorated and ornamented. Coloured paper garlands and chains made of lacquered paper are hung in front of the white sheets covering the walls. In some places, Hungarian Jews decorate their tabernacle or booth *(succa)* with birds made of eggshells with beaks and heads of dough. The booths are also hung with strings of fruits and quotations from the Scriptures. According to belief, on the day of Succot, our forefathers Abraham, Isaac, Jacob, the sons of Jacob, Joseph, Moses, Aaron and King David visit their descendants. In Hungary, a guest-tablet *(ushpizin),* is placed by the entrance to the booth, bearing the names of the forefathers. It is customary to drink toasts to the members of the community who have the above-mentioned names. The toast is called *kiddush,* although *kiddush* is normally the name for the blessing over the wine on Sabbaths and festivals.

On Succot, a special bouquet is made up, consisting of a palm branch, a myrtle sprig, a willow branch and a citrus fruit called an *etrog* (citron). The appropriate prayers are said while holding this bouquet. The etrog resembles a large lemon, and must be totally free of blemishes. It is handled with the utmost care, so it will not break, and once the fruit has been 'used', it is packed in cotton wadding and placed in a special box, which is sometimes made of gold or silver. After the holiday, a jam is made of this fruit, and customarily eaten on 15 Shevat *(Tu bi-Shevat),* the New Year of the Trees, about four months later. On Simhat Torah, the Rejoicing of the Law, all the Torah scrolls are lifted from the Ark and carried in procession around the inside of the synagogue. The children carry flags and sweets are distributed to them.

In Hungary, cabbage is the typical food of this day; stuffed cabbage, cabbage strudel, etc. It is also customary in Hungary from the eve of the New Year until the day of Simhat Torah, when the head of the household blesses the *barhes,* to break off small pieces and dip them in honey.

Days of Atonement

The first two days of the New Year, *Rosh Hashana,* celebrated on the first and second days of Tishri, are also days of repentance and are closely linked to *Yom Kippur,* the Day of Atonement, celebrated on 10 Tishri. The two festivals and the seven days between them are called the Ten Days of Penitence. According to Jewish belief, on the day of Rosh Hashana, the Supreme Judge examines everybody's deeds and pronounces his verdict on the Day of Atonement. Pious Jews prepare for these holidays with great devotion. On the eve of Rosh Hashana, just as on the eve of Yom Kippur, they seek to make peace with their adversaries, they ask the forgiveness of those with whom they have quarrelled and convey their good wishes to each other.

On the eve of Yom Kippur, they declare that all vows and promises made during the year are null and void, so that these should not weigh against them in the eyes of the Heavenly Judgement. This eve has a special name—*Kol Nidre,* meaning 'all vows'. The month preceding the Day of Atonement is spent soul-searching. The blowing of the *shofar,* a ram's horn, every morning serves as a constant reminder.

On the days of Rosh Hashana, sweet dishes dominate the diet, so the New Year will be sweet too. The *barhes,* which on Sabbaths is usually a long braid, is now round, maybe so that the New Year will be round and complete or maybe because the round shape of the bread reminds us of the continuous cycle of life. Poppy seed is sprinkled on top and in Hungary, skilful housewives form birds or roses from the dough and place it on top of the bread before baking. In some places, the *barhes* dough is made with sugar and raisins. On New Year, pieces of the *barhes* are dipped in honey before eating, while on the Sabbath, they are usually dipped in salt.

It is an accepted custom to cook carrots on Rosh Hashana, as they are also sweet. Even if carrots are not eaten, it is considered advisable to look at them, as carrots are associated with fertility; the Yiddish name for carrots is *mehrn,* which sounds like the verb meaning 'to multiply'. According to other interpretations, they symbolize the desire for the multiplication of good deeds.

Poultry is served with the head attached, to express the wish for the participants in the festive meal to become successful during the coming year, because the Hebrew name for the New Year, Rosh Hashana means 'Head of the Year'. In some communities, the innards are not served and the feet of the fowl are thrown away. The final course of the meal is apple compote, apple pie or dessert apples.

The menu served on the eve of the Day of Atonement is identical to that served on the New Year, but because the former is a day of fasting, eating is allowed only before dusk, prior to the start of the festival, and after the end of the 'long day'. On the eve of the festival only light, sparsely-salted dishes are cooked, so that thirst should not disturb the piety of the festival. The strict fast is alleviated in Hungary by snuffing quince jelly with cloves. Smoking is forbidden also, as fire cannot be lit on festivals or the Sabbath, but some Jews get relief by taking snuff.

Children under thirteen are exempted from fasting, as are the sick and nursing mothers. At the end of the fast, a jigger of brandy or liqueur is usually served to prepare those who have fasted for the forthcoming dinner. In some parts of Hungary, dinner consists of coffee with milk, *barhes* and pastries; in other places, chicken paprika is served.

Festivals of Joy

Hanukkah is the Festival of Dedication. It lasts for eight days from 25 Kislev. In 165 B.C.E. the army of Judah the Maccabee won a victory over the pagan Greek rulers of Syria, the Seleucids. After his victory, Judah purified the Temple sanctuary in Jerusalem by removing all the statues which had been erected by the pagans. This is commemorated by Hanukkah. According to tradition, when Judah took over the sanctuary, he found only one cruse of oil that had not been defiled by the pagans. This one cruse, which was needed to keep the Eternal Lamp alight, would have lasted for one day only. However, a miracle occurred: it lasted for eight days, during which time Judah's men were able to obtain the necessary oil. For this reason, in devout Jewish families, the Hanukkah nine-branched candelabra, the *menorah,* is lit; the first night, the *shamash,* the 'servant' candle, is used to light only one candle, then every day one extra candle is lit, until, on the last day, all the candles are lit. A special song is sung for the occasion, the *Ma' oz tzur.* Children are given small presents. They also play with the *trendel* or *dreidel,* a spinning top. On each of the four sides there is a Hebrew letter, indicating whether the player has won or lost. The four letters may be interpreted as the initials of the words, 'a Great Miracle Happened Here', referring to the miracle that occurred in Jerusalem, in 164 B.C.E. In Hungary, Jews also play a card game called *kvitli,* which is basically identical to blackjack or pontoon.

The other day of rejoicing is *Purim*—Feast of Lots. The name comes from the Book of Esther which is read on this day. Haman, a courtier of the Persian King Ahasuerus, plotted to annihilate all the Jews living in the Persian Empire, and by casting lots, he named the fateful day as 13 Adar. His plans were thwarted, because the Jewish Queen Esther saved her people and Haman and his sons were hanged on the scaffold which he had erected for Mordecai, Esther's uncle. The story of Esther is told in the synagogue on the eve of the holiday, and next morning. All listen and rejoice. The highlight of the ceremony is when, during the reading from the scroll containing the Story of Esther, whenever the name of Haman is mentioned, children and adults alike shout and stamp their feet, hit the benches and shake rattles made specially for the occasion. It was also the custom in Hungary for children to write Haman's name on two small tablets and hit each other with the tablets until Haman's name was erased. A life-sized effigy of Haman used to be made and it was either burned or hanged. Dolls of Mordecai and Esther were also made of dough. The so-called 'Purim-rabbi', who was chosen for this day only, was a jester, but one familiar with the Torah; he provided for the amusement of all.

This holiday also always included the *Purimspiel,* a Purim play in the *commedia dell'arte* tradition, recreating the events described in the Book of Esther. The actors used to go from house to house, performing the story; they told of the wisdom of Mordecai, the failure of the evil Haman, and the deliverance of the Jews. The young people put on fancy dress and entertained the celebrants and themselves in carnival atmosphere. It is considered appropriate to drink a lot of wine at Purim, and anyone who drinks so much that he cannot make the distinction between 'Blessed be Mordecai' and 'Cursed be Haman' is considered a true follower of tradition.

In olden times, housewives used to send each other trays filled with pastries and sweets, the *mishbah manot* (*shlahmones* in Yiddish), meaning "the delivering of presents". The housewives used all their ingenuity to outdo each other; they baked a large assortment of pastries and gave and received a lot of cakes and biscuits.

The most popular Purim pastries are the *hamantashen,* three-cornered pastries filled with prune jam or ground poppy seeds, and *lekah,* also called *lekuh, lekeh* or *leikeh,* a honey cake, sometimes made in the image of Esther or Haman, and richly decorated with almonds and raisins. Other favourite pastries are *eierkihli, flodni, kindli,* biscuits, meringues and *krantzli*. In households where baking is important, a so-called *schmatzbaigli* was placed on the tray under the pastries (the recipes for the pastries mentioned in this section will be given later in the book). At Purim, it is customary to eat green vegetables, to signify that Queen Esther remained true to the rituals of her religion, even in the court of King Ahasuerus; she did not eat forbidden foods and kept a strict diet of fruit and vegetables.

Festivals of Mourning

There are numerous days of mourning mentioned in the Jewish calendar, which are also fast days. We shall only deal with one, 9 Av, *Tish'a be-Av* (*Tishebov* in Yiddish). On this day, the Temple in Jerusalem, built by King Solomon, was destroyed by King Nebuchadnezzar in 587 B.C.E. It was rebuilt in 515 B.C.E. and added to by King Herod the Great between 20 and 10 B.C.E. This Second Temple was also destroyed, this time by the Roman Emperor Titus, again on 9 Av. Both of these occasions are mourned on this day.

Even before the day of fasting, from the day of the preceding New Moon, the consumption of meat dishes and wine is forbidden, except on the Sabbath. This period is called the *nayn-tog,* the nine days of milk fast.

Family Celebrations

Family celebrations and important family events play a major role in Jewish culinary tradition. Let us start with *marriage,* which in most cases was arranged by the *shadhan,* the marriage broker.

If the parents, with or without the *shadhan,* came to an arrangement, the bridegroom could visit the bride's family. Later a betrothal ceremony was held, when bridal gifts were presented and a small plate was broken by the fiancé or his future mother-in-law, while the guests greeted the young couple and the parents with shouts of *'mazel tov'* (good luck). The broken pieces of the plate were kept by the fiancée as a lucky charm. The fiancée remained in her parents' home until the wedding day. The date of the wedding was announced by the fiancé in the synagogue on the Sabbath preceding the appointed day, and the women, who traditionally sit in the gallery, would shower him with hazelnuts, almonds, walnuts and sweets as a token of their good wishes. At the end of the Sabbath, the *vorspil* was held, a little informal party for the closest relatives of the bride and groom, so they could get to know each other. The bridegroom's farewell party was held at his home by his friends. *Lekach,* plain biscuits, herring, gefillte fish, fish aspic, wine and brandy were served on this occasion. The bride was also given a farewell party by her friends but it was much less elaborate.

Before the wedding day, both bride and bridegroom immersed themselves in the ritual bath, the *mikvah*. They also fasted before the wedding day, then stepped under the *huppa* (bridal canopy) which was placed in the courtyard of the synagogue. Before the ceremony, honey cake and brandy were eaten by the guests. Then the bride, sitting in a high-backed chair and beautifully attired, received the guests who gave her their blessings. The bride's face was covered with a heavy veil by the bride's mother or, if her mother were dead, by the nearest female relative, called the *unterfirer* in Yiddish, who would lead the veiled bride under the *huppa*. The bridegroom was already there waiting for her with his own *unterfirer* (best man). At that time, the officiating rabbi blessed the couple, read the marriage contract *(ketuba)* aloud, and the couple placed rings on each other's fingers, while saying in Hebrew, 'Be you wedded to me with this ring in accordance with the Laws of Moses and Israel'. Then they both wet their lips from the same wine-filled cup. In very orthodox ceremonies, the bride walked around the bridegroom seven times, as a sign of submission. At the end of the ceremony, a glass or plate was broken; the young husband stepped on the glass or plate, and the broken pieces were picked up and hidden by marriageable girls.

At wedding celebrations, the men and women sat separately, though the couple sat together. The young couple were served first, with a dumpling made of chicken and rice. The next course was usually *goldzip mit fingerhitl,* golden soup with thimble noodles.

Popular wedding dishes were jellied fish, beef broth, roast meat with vegetables, and honey cakes and biscuits. Wine and brandy were also served. Music was provided by Jewish musicians called *klezmorim,* also called Jewish gypsies, who played the violin and sang merry songs. Entertainment was also provided by the *marshelik* (*marshalik* or *bahen*), a jester who told anecdotes, funny stories, jokes and humorous *droshe,* interpretations of the Scriptures. It was also the jester's function to list all presents given to the bride and note who gave them and what their value was; he prompted the guests to dance with the bride and to give her a present. The young husband was supposed to make a short speech; this was sometimes successful, sometimes not, depending on how greatly the bridegroom was embarrassed or how much the guests teased him.

The *mitzva* dance (bridal dance) was performed so that the bride and her dancing partner each held a corner of a handkerchief, as it was forbidden for a man to touch another man's wife.

When the marriage was blessed with a child, at the time of labour, amulets called *kimpet-tsetl* or *kimpet-brivl* were placed on the doors and windows of the expectant mother's room. They contained biblical quotations and incantations against injury.

If a son was born, the father asked someone to be the *kvater* (godfather), which was a great *koved* (honour); it almost established him as a relative. The son, if he was a well-developed, healthy baby, was received into the Covenant of Abraham, i.e. circumcised, when he was eight days old. Circumcision is still performed by the *mohel* (*moil* in Yiddish). On the night before the ceremony, called the *vunacht,* a *minyan,* a quorum of ten adult men stay up all night, eating, drinking and praying.

The circumcision ceremony is followed by the *Se'udah* (*soudeh* in Yiddish), a banquet. Honey cake and *vaiskihli,* sweet white bread, are served, as well as *zoher* peas, peas cooked in salted water and sprinkled with pepper. The word *zoher* in Yiddish comes from the Hebrew *zahar* meaning 'male'. The baby was given a Biblical name, which was sometimes the Hebrew or Yiddish form of his official name. A child could not be named after his parents or a living relative, and a girl could take her mother's name only if the mother died in childbirth.

The birth of a daughter did not require a special ceremony; the father announced her birth in the synagogue and a name was given to her in front of the Torah. After the religious service, a small party with wine *(kiddush)* was held.

While the mother was recuperating from childbirth, relatives, neighbours, or the *kvater*'s wife helped in the household. During this period, visitors would call with many delicious foods and cakes. As the months and years passed and the male child grew up and reached the age of four or five, his father took him to the *heder,* Jewish elementary school, where the *melamed,* the teacher, gave him instruction in Hebrew reading, writing and basic religious education. He was introduced to the Five Books of Moses, the *humash.* When the child attended school for the first time, his mother made him pastries from honey dough in the shape of the *alef-bes,* the alphabet, which he gave to the other children. On other days, the child took with him a so-called *parve* cake (*parve* means a dish containing neither meat nor milk products, so it can be eaten at any meal) and a hard-boiled egg (also *parve*).

At thirteen, a boy becomes *Bar Mitzvah* (Son of the Commandments), in other words, he becomes a man, and all the Jewish commandments *(mitzvot)* are his responsibility now. At the ceremony held on this occasion—usually on the Sabbath—he is called on to read the portion of the Torah (the Scrolls of the Law) for the coming week. The Bar Mitzvah boy is given valuable presents by his parents, his relatives and especially his *kvater*. The presents are usually a *tallit* (*talles* in Yiddish, a prayer shawl) and *tefillin* (phylacteries). On this occasion, a boy usually received his first watch, gold ring, etc. The guests are treated to a lot of delicacies often cooked by the boy's mother. Naturally, poorer families celebrated the Bar Mitzvah less elaborately, by only giving a simple *kiddush* and serving cold fish and cakes to the guests.

Barley Soup

When a close relative dies, an intensive period of mourning lasting seven days is observed. This is called the *shiva*, meaning seven. At this time, relatives and good neighbours provide sustenance for the mourners who must not do their own cooking. The first food eaten by mourners after the funeral is a hard-boiled egg sprinkled with ashes. The mourners sit on low stools; all the mirrors in the house are covered over and each mourner has a piece of clothing ritually torn by the rabbi. Prayers are held on each of the seven days at the house. The corpse is not present, because, for reasons of hygiene, Jewish funerals take place as soon as possible after death.

RITUAL PRESCRIPTIONS

We have already mentioned that ritual requirements have played an important role in the development of traditional Jewish cooking, inasmuch as there are numerous, otherwise common foods of animal origin that can not be found in a Jewish kitchen. One of the first things we wish to discuss is the food that Jews are permitted to eat.

The dietary laws are religious in origin, but they incorporate concepts of sound hygiene and the protection of nature. Even the rules for fasting contain up-to-date nutritional requirements. The prohibitions and taboos governing eating are to be found in Leviticus and Deuteronomy. The XIVth chapter of Deuteronomy states which animals are clean, and therefore edible, and which are unclean and must not be eaten.

If someone partakes of the flesh of a forbidden animal, he has to go through a process of ritual cleansing. According to the law, clean animals are the ox, the sheep, the goat, the fallow deer, the roebuck, the wild goat, the antelope, the wild ox, and the chamois; in other words, all ruminants with cloven hooves (Deut. XIV: 5–6). It is forbidden to eat the camel, the hare and the rabbit (Deut. XIV: 7). However, the greatest taboo is against eating the pig, whose flesh may not even be touched (Deut. XIV: 8). Other unclean animals are those that walk on uncloven hooves, such as the horse, the donkey and the mule. The following birds are forbidden: vultures, eagles, kites, swallows, swans and storks. All flying and crawling insects are forbidden. Animals that are otherwise clean can not be eaten if they are found dead. It is strictly forbidden to partake of the blood of animals. Among fish, only those with true scales and fins may be eaten.

Neighbouring nations had systems of dietary laws similar to those of the Jews. The laws of Moses reevaluated these taboos and made them the laws of God. The so-called clean animals could be consumed only if they were slaughtered by a *shohet,* a ritual slaughterer, who then pronounced the meat *kosher,* or fit to be eaten.

The opposite of kosher is *teref* (*treifeh* in Yiddish, or *trefli* in Hungarian-Jewish parlance). This literally means 'carrion', but has come to mean any forbidden food or unclean utensil. The *shohet* first examines the animal to see whether it is fit for slaughter. Care is taken that the animal's suffering should be minimal. The *haaf,* the ritual knife, must have a completely smooth, sharp blade. The animal's jugular vein, trachaea and esophagus are severed with one sharp cut. The jugular vein is severed in order to drain the blood from the carcass. The slaughtered animal's entrails are examined; it is forbidden to eat the flesh of a deformed, damaged or diseased animal.

The slaughtered animal then has to be cleaned; in the case of fowl, all the feathers have to be removed. Using the dry method, the feathers of the fowls are singed by holding it under a flame lit from a spill; the blood under the skin must not be allowed to cook. Nor must the meat be washed in hot water for the same reason, but always in cold. The skin has to be carefully scraped, then the animal is cut up. The following order must be observed: first the head and feet are cut off, then beaks and claws have to be removed. Next the head is split in half; the fork-shaped *trefe* bone is discarded and the brain and eyes are removed. This is followed by removal of the four *trefe* veins from the neck. For safety's sake, the neck has to be cut in several places. Now the wings are removed, then the inside is opened and the intestines, liver, heart and gizzard are removed. The liver must be handled with care, the tip of the heart and the thick part of the gizzard have to be cut off. The fat is removed from the stomach cavity, or if it is liquid, it has to be koshered later, after removal of the appendix. If an egg is found in a fowl, it has to be koshered separately and this egg can be eaten in meat dishes only. Nowadays, most red meat is already koshered before reaching the housewife.

Koshering consists of the following. *Utensils:* a large bowl, a work surface, bucket, dipper, a wicker basket or pierced board, a deep bowl, coarse salt, kosher soap and towels.

The bowl is placed on the work surface and the meat is put into it. The meat is covered with running water taken from the bucket, using the dipper. The meat remains in this water for half an hour. Then the meat is removed and placed in the wicker basket or on the pierced board, under which the other bowl is placed. The meat is now carefully dried, in preparation for salting. The pieces of meat are salted with coarse dry salt. All the surfaces and cavities have to be salted carefully. The salt is left on the meat for an hour, then it is shaken off and the meat is rinsed in still water three times. Now it is ready for cooking and eating. The utensils used in koshering have to be washed and rinsed at least three times and can be used only for this purpose. Liver would be ruined by salting, so it is koshered by searing under or over a naked flame, taking care not to burn it.

A kosher kitchen requires many dishes and utensils. Completely separate dishes, utensils, towels and dishwashing equipment are used for meat dishes, and those containing meat products. In a Jewish kitchen the two sets of equipment cannot be together at any time. Many kitchens use separate sinks for milk and meat, and separate refrigerator shelves.

There are foods that can be consumed without restrictions. These are called *parve* foods, also called *parosh* in Hungary, and contain neither milk nor meat. Meat and milk dishes cannot be eaten at the same meal, as they are not supposed to mix in one's stomach. As meat takes longer to be digested than milk, one has to wait longer after eating meat than after eating milk-based dishes.

The utensils used for cooking *parve* foods, such as fish and eggs, are stored separately. The pastry-board, rolling-pin and kneading bowl are also kept in a separate place. In the kitchen cabinets, the following order should be observed:

The bottom cabinets should contain the pots, pans, baking tins and pot lids; the drawers should contain the cutlery, and the upper wall cabinets the spices, flour, breadcrumbs, *barhes* crumbs, sugar, etc., and all the utensils used for koshering, the washing-up bowls and dishcloths. All the milk and meat utensils are stored separately from each other; milk utensils are marked in blue, and meat in red.

In summary, the basic rule of the Jewish kitchen is that the flesh of clean animals and fowl can be eaten only if slaughtered in the ritual manner and if the housewife removes all the blood by salting and soaking the meat in water, and serving food in special dishes according to a strictly-observed combination of foods.

Please note!
The recipes in this book are for 4 servings.

Foods of Vegetable Origin

The most important foodstuff of vegetable origin is bread. There are many others in the Hungarian-Jewish diet, including salad plants, herbs, fruits, potatoes, rice, barley, pasta, carrots, parsley, celery, beets, beans, peas, lentils, sweetcorn, onions, garlic, paprika, etc. In this respect, it differs only slightly from the commonly used ingredients, though there is a tendency to avoid vegetables that cannot be cleaned thoroughly, for fear they might still contain insects, when brought to table. The Bible mentions bread frequently. It was usually leavened, but for some ceremonial occasions unleavened bread was baked. The round loaves were baked in ovens or on hot stones.

Bread and Challah (Barhes)

To make household bread, sift 2 kg (4¼ lb) of flour into a bowl. Make a well in the centre, and add either a yeast starter, as described below in the *barhes* recipe, or a mixture of 1 tablespoon fresh yeast, 1 teaspoon sugar and 250 ml (8 fl oz) lukewarm water, having left the mixture in a warm place for 20 minutes to foam. Gradually combine the mixture with the flour, then add 1 teaspoon of salt, and enough lukewarm water to make a smooth, firm dough, about 1 litre (1¾ pints). Knead the dough until it is smooth and elastic and no longer sticks to your fingers. Then shape the dough into round loaves and place them in a basket lined with a well-floured cloth. Cover and leave it to rise for 90 minutes or until doubled in bulk. Break off a piece of dough and throw it in the fire, as is done for *challah*. Shape the bread into four loaves and leave them to prove for 45 minutes on floured baking sheets. Bake the loaves in a preheated hot oven (200 °C, 400 °F, Gas Mark 6) for 1 hour or until the tops are golden-brown and the bread sounds hollow when the base is rapped with the knuckles.

Bread can also be made with a yeast starter (see below). To make *barhes:* Sift 1.5 kg (3¼ lb) bread flour into a bowl. Make a well in the centre and add 25 g (1 oz) 1 tablespoon fresh yeast dissolved with 100 ml (4 fl oz) lukewarm water and 2 teaspoons sugar. Take 2 potatoes, boiled, peeled and mashed, and beat them into the mixture with 1 teaspoon salt. Knead the dough, adding 2 tablespoons oil and enough water to make it smooth and elastic. Leave it to rise, covered with a damp cloth, in a warm place for two hours.

When the dough has risen, break off a piece and throw it in the fire. Divide the dough into 3 parts and braid it, and either leave it as an oblong or coil it up. Let it prove for half an hour. Before baking, brush it with beaten egg and sprinkle it with poppy seeds. *Barhes* prepared for a festival should be decorated according to taste. For weddings and joyous occasions, the *barhes* is split into multiple braids and brushed with sugar and water before baking; afterwards, it is sprinkled with poppy-seeds. Four *barhes* are prepared for the Sabbath. Two are eaten on Friday night, and two are blessed at the Sabbath midday meal and eaten then and later.

In less affluent Jewish communities, where they could not afford to bake wheaten bread for everyday consumption, they made *karsht* from cornmeal.

2 kg (4¼ lb) cornmeal was mixed with the starter and a teaspoon of salt and left to rise in a well-oiled baking tin for 2 hours. Then it was baked like household bread.

The yeast starter is made from 45 g (1¾ oz) fresh yeast, mixed with 300 g (10 oz) bread flour and enough water to make a mixture the consistency of thick cream. This is left overnight to ferment and added to the bread the next day.

SOUPS

Beef Soup

600–700 g (1¼–1½ lb) koshered lean beef, 2–3 beef bones, a small piece of marrow-bone, 2 medium-sized carrots, 1 good-sized parsley root (or parsnip), 1 small piece of kohlrabi, one medium-sized onion, 5–6 cloves of garlic, a handful of haricot beans, salt, 5–6 black peppercorns, a small amount of paprika, 3 litres (5 pints) of cold water

Place the meat in a bowl while you prepare the vegetables. Soak the white beans for a couple of hours or more. Leave the cleaned vegetables in another bowl until they are to be cooked. Fasten the marrow-bone with a string so that the marrow will not slip out during cooking. Pour the water into the saucepan, then carefully add the bones, the marrow-bone and the meat and start cooking over a low heat. Remove all the froth as it rises to the surface, so that you get a nice clear soup. As the meat starts to become tender, add the vegetables and seasonings. When the meat is tender, remove it and the vegetables from the soup and strain into a warmed tureen.

Chicken Soup

1 medium-sized koshered chicken, 3 large carrots, 2 parsley roots (or 2 parsnips), one medium-sized celeriac, 1 large onion, 5–6 garlic cloves, salt, 7–8 peppercorns, 3 litres (5 pints) of cold water

Put the chicken into a pan of cold water and start cooking over a low heat. When the contents begin to boil, skim off any froth that rises to the surface. When the chicken starts to become tender, after 1 hour, add all the remaining ingredients and continue to simmer until they are all cooked, at least another hour. Strain the soup and serve.
Note! Goose, duck or turkey soup is prepared in the same manner.

Bouillon

200 g (7 oz) beef bones, 400 g (14 oz) koshered lean beef or half a koshered chicken (or the feet, wings and giblets of a koshered chicken), 1 carrot, 1 parsley root or parsnip, 1 stick celery, 1 tsp tomato purée, 2–3 black peppercorns, salt, 1½ litres (2½ pints) water, and 1 egg yolk for each person

Place the meat in the water and start to simmer it over a very low heat. Skim off all the froth as it rises to the surface. Place the bones and the cleaned and diced vegetables in a roasting tin and brown in a medium oven until golden. Add the seasonings to the clear stock, and continue to simmer. Blend the tomato purée with a little soup and add at the very end. Continue to simmer the meat for at least three hours. Remove the bones, the meat and the vegetables, then strain the soup. Add one egg yolk per person before serving, taking care that the yolks do not break.

Goldzip—Golden Soup
for a wedding

1 large koshered boiling fowl, 3–4 medium-sized carrots, 3–4 parsley roots (or parsnips), 1 medium-sized onion, salt, 7–8 black peppercorns, 1 tsp saffron, 3 litres (5 pints) cold water

Proceed as in the recipe above, but just before the soup is ready, add the saffron to give the soup its golden colour.

Goulash Soup

500 g (1 lb) lean koshered beef, 2 tbs goose fat, 1 large onion, 2 garlic cloves, 1 tsp paprika, 1 tsp tomato purée, salt, a pinch of caraway seeds, 1 sweet pepper, 1 tomato, 1 small carrot, 1 small parsley root (or parsnip), 4–5 large potatoes, 1 litre (1¾ pints) water

Cut the meat into small cubes. Chop the onions finely and brown them in the goose fat. Add the finely chopped garlic and paprika, and stir well. Add the cubed meat, stir, then add the salt and the caraway seeds.
Add 225 ml (8 fl oz) water and simmer over a low heat. Add the vegetables, paprika, tomato, tomato purée and the diced or julienned potatoes. More water may be added according to taste.

Sauce Accompaniments to Meat Dishes

Garlic Soup I

3–4 garlic cloves, peeled, 2 tbs goose fat or oil, 2 tbs plain flour, a small amount of paprika, salt, 1 litre (1¾ pints) lukewarm water

Crush the garlic to a purée. Brown the flour in goose fat or oil, taking care not to burn it. Stir in the puréed garlic, add salt and paprika. Mix thoroughly. Gently add the lukewarm water and bring to simmering point.

Garlic Soup II

3–4 garlic cloves, 1 tsp plain flour, a pinch of salt, pepper, paprika, 1½ litres (2½ pints) of water in which potatoes have been cooked

Chop or crush the garlic finely. Cream it with the salt, pepper, and paprika, then stir in a small amount of potato water, slowly adding all the rest. Bring to simmering point.

Krotzip—Cabbage Soup I

1 small head of cabbage, 1 tsp salt, 1 small onion, 2 tbs oil or goose fat, 2 tbs flour, 1 litre (1¾ pints) of water

Make a thin, light roux of the fat and flour by cooking them together in a saucepan, stirring constantly. Stir in and brown the onions. Cut the cabbage lengthwise and cook until tender in a small amount of water. Take a small amount of liquid from the pan in which the cabbage was cooked and add it to the roux, then stir the mixture into the cabbage soup. Bring to simmering point and serve.

Krotzip—Cabbage Soup II

2 litres (3½ pints) cabbage stock, 1 medium head soured cabbage, 1 tbs goose fat or oil, 1 tbs flour, 1 small onion, 2–3 garlic cloves, 200–300 g (7–11 oz) sauerkraut, 200 g (7 oz) smoked goose, beef or pastrami

Make a light, thin roux by cooking the fat and flour together, stirring constantly. Grate the onions, chop or crush the garlic and stir them in the roux. Slowly add the cabbage stock. Add the koshered meat and continue cooking until tender, about 1 hour.

Dairy Tomato Soup

1 tsp butter, 1 tsp flour, 500 ml (16 fl oz) tomato juice, 225 ml (8 fl oz) milk, salt, 1 tsp sugar

Lightly brown the flour in the butter, stir in a small amount of water and add the tomato juice. Add salt and sugar to taste. Slowly stir in the milk and heat until boiling.

Beetroot Borscht

2 large raw beetroots, salt, 1 litre (1¾ pints) of water, a few drops of lemon juice, a pinch of black pepper, 1 egg yolk per person, sour cream to taste (optional)

Peel and grate the beetroots coarsely. Cook them in the water until tender, about 15 minutes. Add the salt, lemon juice and pepper. When serving, place an egg yolk into each soup bowl, strain the beetroot juice over it and add the pieces of beetroot. Sour cream may be added according to taste. Usually it is served with boiled potatoes to make a more filling meal.

Beetroot Borscht
for Passover

Proceed as above, but use pickled beetroots *(rissel)* that have been prepared after Purim.

Barley Soup I

2 tbs goose fat or oil, 2 tbs plain flour, 2 tbs pearl barley per person, 2–3 garlic cloves, 1 small carrot, chopped, 1 parsley root (or parsnip), chopped, salt, a pinch of paprika, a pinch of ground black pepper, 1 litre (1¾ pints) of water

Chop or crush the garlic. Heat the fat and mix in the flour, stirring constantly, and add half the water. Cook the barley for 15 minutes. Add the garlic and the barley. Cook the chopped vegetables in the rest of the water. When the barley is tender, about 25 minutes, add the strained water to the roux, pour the mixture back on to the barley and simmer.

Barley Soup II

1 litre (1¾ pint) beef stock, 200 g (7 oz) pearl barley, salt, a pinch of paprika, pinch of ground black pepper

Rinse the barley. Cook it until tender in the beef stock and season to taste.

Fishroe Soup
for Friday lunch

400 g (14 oz) fish heads, fish trimmings and roe, 1 litre (1¾ pints) of water, 1 carrot, 1 parsley root (or 1 parsnip), 2–3 potatoes, 3 small onions, 1 tbs plain flour, 2–3 tbs oil or 50–60 g (1–1½ oz) butter, 1 bunch of parsley, a pinch of paprika, ground black pepper, salt, 2 bay leaves, a few drops of vinegar

Season the fish with salt. Dice the vegetables and throw them into boiling water. While the vegetables are cooking, make a thin, light roux with the flour, butter and finely chopped onions. When the roux starts to brown, add the parsley, the seasonings and the fish. Slowly add the potato and vegetable broth and stir till smooth, while bringing it to the simmering point. Season with a few drops of vinegar. Add the fish and bay leaves. When the fish is cooked through, about 15 minutes, carefully remove it discarding the bones, and return the fish to the broth. Just before serving, season again with a few drops of vinegar and return the vegetables to the soup.

Fish Soup with Sour Cream or Egg Yolks

2 medium-sized onions, 1 tbs butter, 1 tsp flour, a pinch of paprika, salt, 250 ml (16 fl oz) water, 400 g (14 oz) fish heads, fish trimmings and roe, 500 ml (16 fl oz) sour cream or 2 egg yolks

Finely chop the onions. Blend the flour and butter over low heat. Add the onions and continue to brown the mixture, then add the seasonings and water, and stir until smooth. Finally add the fish and simmer. When the fish is tender, remove and bone it, return the fish to the pan and cook for 5 minutes. Before serving, remove from the heat, stir in the sour cream or the egg yolks, beaten with 125 ml (4 fl oz) of the soup.

Almond Soup

225 ml (8 fl oz) milk, 1 vanilla pod, 100 g (4 oz) blanched, ground almonds, 4 egg yolks, 2 tbs sugar

Cook the vanilla pod, almonds, and sugar in the milk over low heat, until the mixture comes to the boil. When it has cooled, add 225 ml (8 fl oz) of the liquid to the egg yolks and slowly pour this back into the pan.

SOUP GARNISHES

Kreplach

for New Year, Yom Kippur Eve, the Seventh Day of Tabernacles, and Purim

For the dough: *175 g (6 oz) flour, 1 egg, 1–2 tbs water, pinch of salt, 1 egg white*
For the filling: *150–200 g (6–7 oz) minced meat (cooked or raw), ground black pepper, 1 egg, 3 sprigs of parsley, finely chopped*

Combine the flour, egg, salt and the water and knead the firm dough until it is smooth and elastic. Cover with clingfilm and leave in the refrigerator for at least 30 minutes. Meanwhile mix all the filling ingredients together. Roll out the dough until very thin. Put small mounds of filling on the dough at regular intervals, then cover it with the other half of rolled-out dough. Press down firmly between the mounds. Brush with egg white to seal it completely. Cut the dough into small pieces with a ravioli cutter. Cook in boiling water for 10 minutes. Serve with a beef soup.

Lung Kreplach

For the dough: *200 g (7 oz) flour, 1 egg, 2 tbs water, a pinch of salt*
For the filling: *200 g (7 oz) calf's lungs, 3 tbs goose fat or oil, 1 small onion, salt, 1 tsp ground black pepper, 1 egg*

Mix the flour, salt, egg and water and knead to a smooth, elastic dough. Leave it to stand, then roll the dough to a medium thickness.
For the filling: Cook the calf's lungs in salted water and mince them. Brown the finely chopped onions in oil or fat, add the salt and pepper and continue browning. Add the minced lung. Allow the mixture to cool, then stir in the egg. Proceed as in the recipe above. Cook the kreplach in boiling soup.

Knaidlach (Matzo Balls) I
for Passover

4 eggs, water, 4 tbs goose fat, 1 tsp salt, a pinch of ground black pepper, a pinch of ground ginger, 225 g (8 oz) matzo meal, 1 whole matzo

Break the eggs into a large bowl, add an equal amount of water, add the melted goose fat and spices, then gently stir in the matzo meal and the soaked matzo. Set aside for an hour. Wet your hands with cold water, take a small amount of mixture and roll it into a walnut-sized ball between your palms. Drop the matzo balls into simmering hot soup.
Note! The matzo balls tend to soak up a lot of liquid.

Knaidlach (Matzo Balls) II
for Passover

2 eggs, 4 tbs water, 2 tbs oil or goose fat, salt, ground black pepper, ground ginger, matzo meal

Follow the recipe above, using just enough matzo meal to obtain a soft mixture. The mixture should be left to rest for at least one hour. Wet your hands with cold water, take a small amount of mixture and roll it into small balls between your palms. Cook the matzo balls covered, in hot soup.

Cooked Potato Kugel I
for Passover

2 eggs, 2 tbs goose fat or oil, 2 tbs cooked, mashed potatoes, 1 tbs water, salt, ground black pepper, ground ginger, matzo meal

Combine the eggs with the melted goose fat or oil, water and spices; add the mashed potatoes and blend until smooth. Stir in as much matzo meal as needed to get an easily manageable dough. Wet your hands with cold water, and roll the dough into small balls. Cook them in boiling soup.

Cooked Potato Kugel II
for Passover

3 cold boiled potatoes, 3 eggs, matzo meal, 2 tbs goose fat or oil, salt, ground black pepper

Coarsely grate the cooked potatoes and mix them with the eggs, melted goose fat, salt, and pepper. Add sufficient matzo meal to produce an easily manageable dough. Let it rest for an hour, then, using wet hands, roll the mixture into small balls. Cook them in boiling soup.

Dumplings (Spaetzli)
for Passover

3 eggs, 3–4 tbs matzo meal, salt

Whisk the egg yolks with the salt and matzo meal until smooth, fold in the stiffly beaten egg whites. Let the batter rest for a while, then drop small spoonfuls of it into boiling soup.

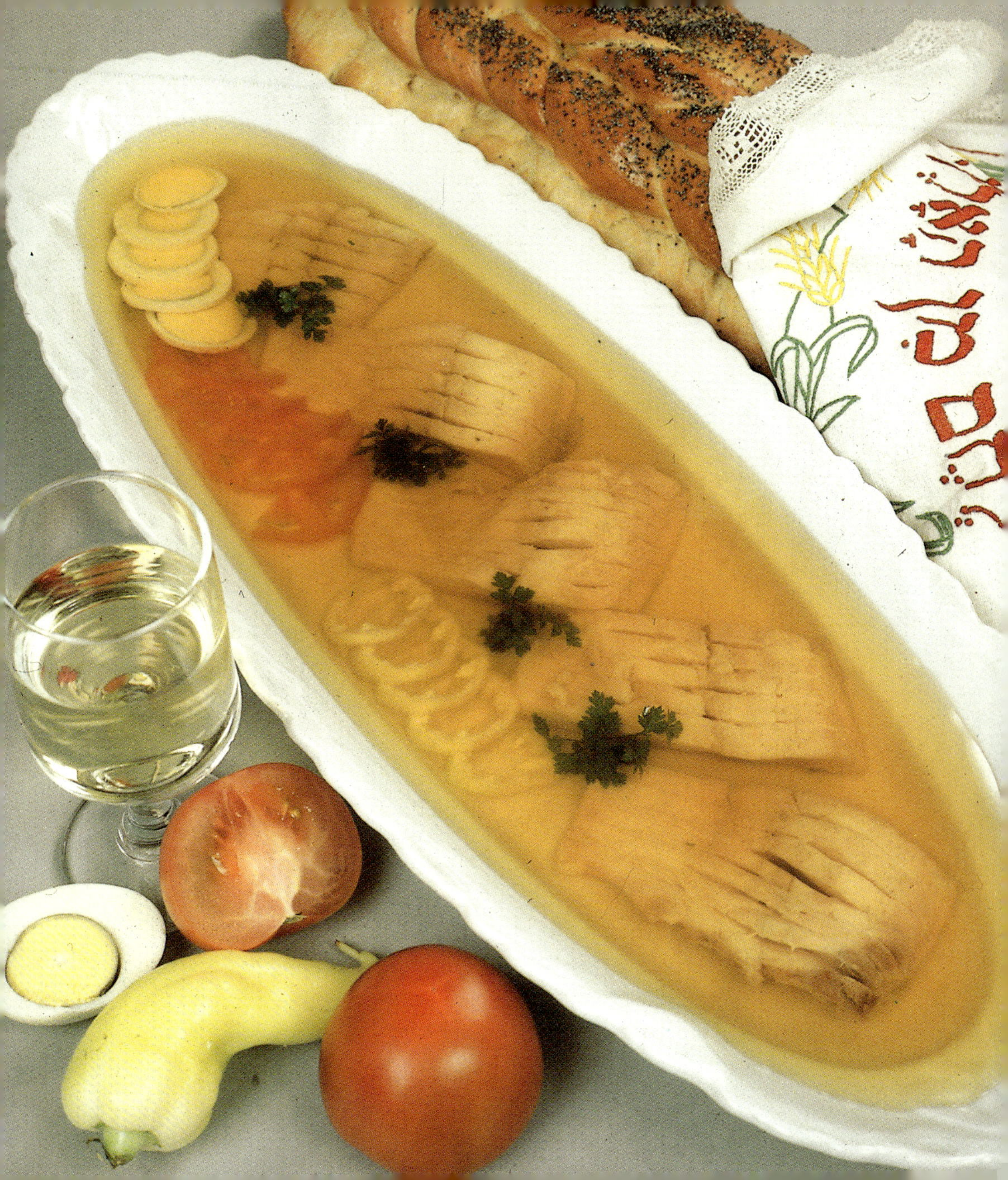

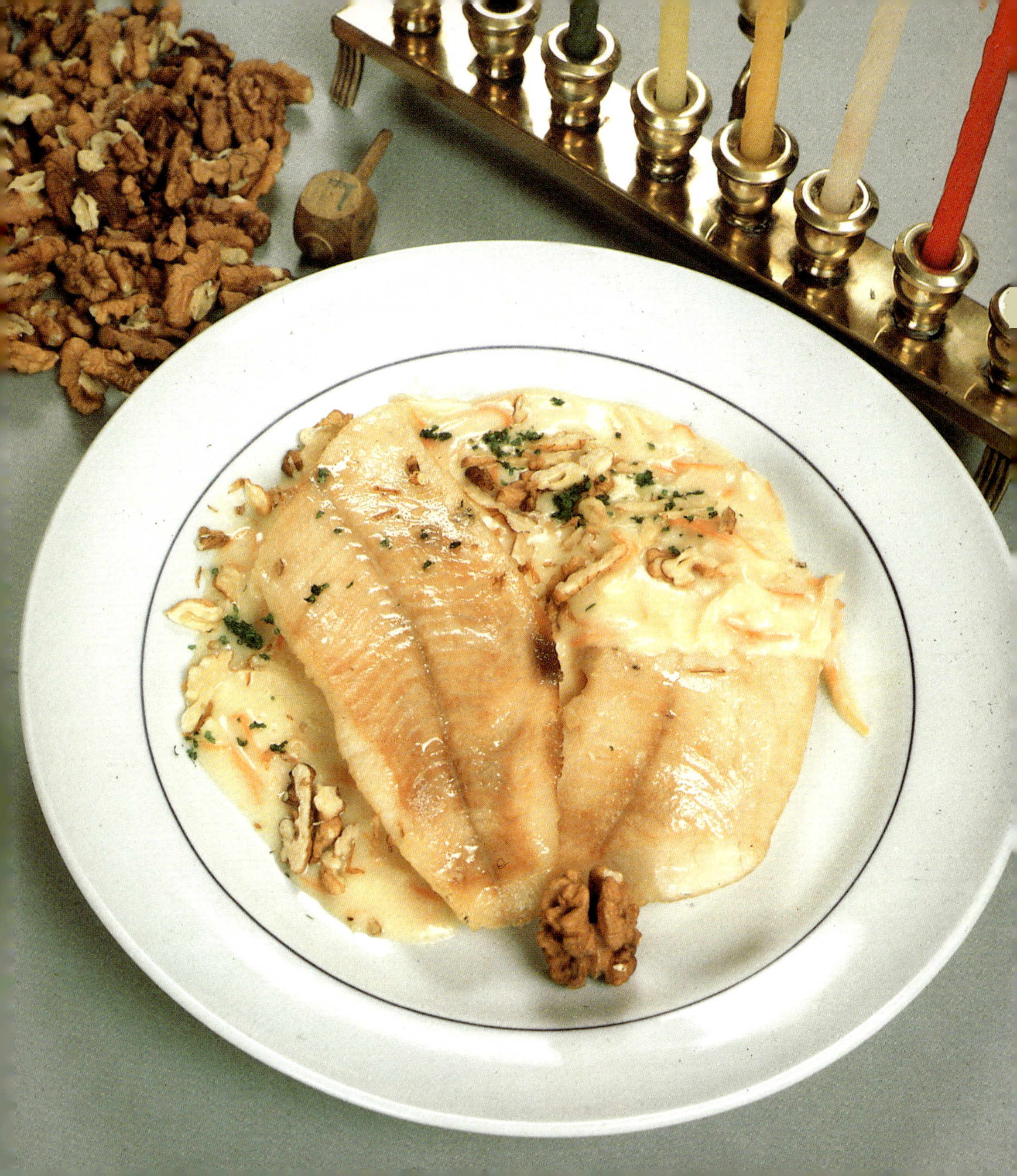

SAUCES

Apple Sauce

2 tbs goose fat or oil, 3–4 medium-sweet apples, peeled and diced, 2 tbs plain flour, stock

Melt the fat and put the apples into it. Cook until they are lightly browned. Sprinkle the apples with flour and add the stock, taking care not to let lumps form. Bring to the boil and simmer for 3 to 5 minutes.

Cucumber Sauce with Raisins
for New Year

7–8 small sweet pickled gherkins, 2 tbs goose fat or oil, 2 tbs plain flour, a handful of raisins, 1 tsp sugar or honey, 300 ml (½ pint) stock

Make a light roux by heating together the fat and flour. Stir in the cubed gherkins, add the washed and soaked raisins, and finally stir in enough stock to make a thick sauce after simmering for 3 to 5 minutes. Sweeten the sauce with sugar or honey according to taste.

Raisin Sauce
for New Year

2 tbs plain flour, 2 tbs goose fat, 2–3 tbs lemon juice (optional), sugar, 100 g (4 oz) raisins

Wash and soak the raisins in water or chicken stock. Make a light, thin roux, add the washed and soaked raisins and enough water to make a thick sauce. Sweeten with sugar to taste and simmer together for 3 to 5 minutes. Lemon juice may be added to give extra flavour.

Pike Stuffed with Walnuts

Chestnut Sauce
for New Year

500 g (18 oz) chestnuts, 3–4 tbs goose fat or oil, 3–4 tbs plain flour, salt, 1 tbs sugar, stock

Make a slit in the skin of the chestnuts and after soaking them in water, roast them in the oven. Remove the inner and outer skins, and push the chestnuts through a potato-ricer, or grind in a food-processor, reserving a few chestnuts for garnish. Make a thin, light sauce, add the chestnut mixture, sugar, salt, and enough stock to make a thick sauce. Heat the sauce and add the whole chestnuts.

Sour-cherry Sauce

500 g (18 oz) morello cherries, 3–4 tbs goose fat or oil, 3–4 tbs plain flour, 2 tsp sugar, cloves, a pinch of ground cinnamon, 400 ml (14 fl oz) stock

Stir the cooked and stoned sour cherries in fat or oil. Sprinkle them gently with the flour and add the cloves, cinnamon and sugar. Add the stock, taking care not to form lumps. Bring the sauce to the boil and add a little water if required.

Horse-radish Sauce with Raisins

3–4 tbs goose fat or oil, 4 tbs plain flour, 50 g (2 oz) raisins, 1 tsp sugar, 1 medium (10 cm/4 in) horse-radish, a pinch of salt, stock

Grate the cleaned horse-radish. Make a light, thin roux using the flour and fat, add some stock, sugar, salt and the washed, soaked raisins. Finally add the grated horse-radish, bring to the boil and serve boiling hot.

ACCOMPANIMENTS

Millet

500 g (18 oz) husked millet, 4–5 tbs goose fat or oil, a small onion, salt, water

Brown the chopped onions in fat or oil, stir in the washed millet, brown, and add enough water to cover it. Add salt and cook over a low heat. If the water evaporates, keep adding more until the millet is tender.

Prunes with Rice

250 g (9 oz) prunes, 6–8 handfuls of rice, a koshered goose, salt

Wash the prunes in warm water, then cook them in a cup of water until tender. Brown the cleaned and washed rice and add the water, the washed goose, salt and cook until the rice and meat are tender. Keep replacing any evaporated water. Finally add the cooked prunes.

Cabbage with Beans

1 small head of cabbage, 500 g (18 oz) shelled broad beans, 3–4 garlic cloves, 3–4 tbs goose fat, 3–4 tbs plain flour, salt, 1 tsp pepper

Cook the thinly sliced cabbage and the washed beans separately. Make a light, thin roux, add the pressed garlic and finally, stir in the cooked beans and cabbage. Add salt and pepper.

Barley with Fried Onion

500 g (18 oz) barley, 4–5 tbs goose fat, a large onion, 1 litre (1¾ pints) water

Clean and wash the barley, brown in 3 tablespoons of the fat, add the water and cook until tender. Brown the sliced onions in the rest of the fat and sprinkle over the barley.

Farvli or Ferfli (Farfel) with Stuffed Neck
for Sabbath

For the farfel barley: *1 egg, 200 g (7 oz) plain flour, salt, 1 tbs water*
For the rest: *the skin of a goose's neck (or use 2 chicken necks), 200 g (7 oz) flour, 1 parsley root (or parsnip), 1 carrot, 1 onion, a little goose fat, salt, pepper, paprika*

Knead the eggs, flour and a small amount of water into a smooth firm dough. Let it dry, then grate and spread it out on a baking sheet to allow it to dry further. Make a filling of the flour, fat, paprika, pepper and salt and stuff it into the skin. Sew up the ends with white thread or close the necks using a skewer.
Clean and slice the vegetables, and steam them together with the stuffed goose neck. Meanwhile brown the barley in a small amount of goose fat until golden, add the water and cook until tender. Place the stuffed goose neck and vegetables on top of the egg barley and serve.

Potato Kugel

Per person: *2 large potatoes, 1 egg, 1 tbs goose fat, plain flour, salt, ground black pepper*

Boil the potatoes in their skins, peel and mash well, add the goose fat, salt, pepper, and if the mixture is too thin, add a little flour so that it can be shaped into little balls. Cook the kugel in boiling water, serve with game or meat stews.

Tsimmes

2 tbs goose fat, 50 g (2 oz) barley, salt, ground black pepper, nutmeg, 1 small carrot, 1 large potato, a pinch of sugar

Stir the washed barley in the hot goose fat until golden brown. Add the water, salt, pepper and nutmeg. Peel the potato, slice the carrot and cook them together with the barley. Sugar may be added to taste.

Split Peas
for Circumcision celebrations

Per person: *200 g (7 oz) split peas, salt, ground black pepper*

After cleaning and washing the split peas, cook them in water until tender. Let them cool and add the salt and pepper.

Layered Potatoes

1 kg (2¼ lb) potatoes, 1 small onion, 6–7 hard-boiled eggs, 50–60 g (2–2½ oz) butter, 225 ml (8 fl oz) sour cream, salt

Boil the washed potatoes in their skins, peel and slice them thinly. Slice the hard-boiled eggs. Butter a large pot liberally. Arrange the potatoes and the eggs in alternate layers, placing the chopped onions on top of the eggs. Finish with a top layer of potatoes. Pour melted butter and sour cream over the top. Bake in the oven at 180 °C (350 °F, Gas Mark 4) for an hour until cooked and golden brown on top.

VEGETABLES

Carrots
for New Year

3 large carrots, 2 tbs goose fat or oil, 1 tbs plain flour, 4 tbs honey or sugar, about 300 ml (½ pint) water or stock

Stir the cleaned and sliced carrots in the hot fat, add honey and simmer slowly until tender. Then let all the water evaporate, taking care not to burn the carrots. Gently sprinkle with the flour and add water or stock. Simmer for about 3 minutes until the flour is cooked.

Green Beans

Per person: 200 g (7 oz) green beans, 1 tsp sugar, 1 tbs goose fat or oil, 2–3 pieces of fruit in season: apples, anchovies, plums (stoned), 1 tbs plain flour

Cook the cleaned and diced beans in salted water. While the beans are cooking, stew the fruit in a small amount of water, adding sugar to taste. When the beans are tender, make a thin roux adding some of the water in which the beans were cooked. Stir until smooth and add the beans and fruit.

Cinnamon Apples

3–4 apples, 25 g (1 oz) butter, 2 tbs plain flour, 1 tbs sugar, a small piece of cinnamon, 1 tbs sour cream

Peel the apples and cut them into thin slices. Sprinkle the flour over the melted butter, add the apple slices, sprinkle with a mixture of sugar and cinnamon. When serving, add some sour cream. Serve with milk dishes.

Stuffed Cabbage

500 g (18 oz) sauerkraut, 5–6 cabbage leaves, 1 large and 1 small onion, 2 tbs goose fat, ½ breast of koshered goose, 1 piece of fat unrendered goose 300–400 g (11–15 oz) koshered beef shoulder, 200 g (7 oz) rice, 1 egg, 3–4 garlic cloves, 500 ml (¾ pint) tomato juice, 2 tbs plain flour, a pinch of paprika, salt, ground black pepper

Rinse the sauerkraut in cold water according to taste. Fry the thinly sliced large onion until golden in the 2 tablespoonfuls of hot goose fat in a large, heavy saucepan, then add most of the sauerkraut. Meanwhile prepare the *filling:* Mince together the beef, goose meat and solid goose fat. Grate the small onion. Mix the minced onion with one clove of garlic, salt, pepper and the egg. Stir in the washed rice. Mix well. Stuff the cabbage leaves with part of the filling. Make small balls from the rest. Place the cabbage bundles and meat balls on top of the sauerkraut-onion mixture and cover with the remaining sauerkraut. Add enough water to cover. Start cooking over a low heat. Meanwhile prepare a roux, adding the rest of the garlic, the paprika, and the tomato juice. Stir the roux into the cabbage, but first remove the cabbage-bundles and meat balls, and let all the water evaporate. Finally, place the cabbage bundles back into the pan and simmer. Add sugar to taste.

Cholent I

500 g (18 oz) white beans, 1 large onion, 2–3 garlic cloves, 1 smoked koshered goose leg or breast, 200 g (7 oz) koshered brisket, salt

Wash and soak the beans in water overnight. Put half the beans in a deep earthenware casserole or Dutch oven. Add the meat, the goose leg, then the rest of the beans and finally add the minced garlic and finely chopped onions. Cover with water. You may place the kugel on top and cook it together with the cholent.
The kugel has many variations (see on the next page).

Cholent II

500 g (18 oz) white beans, 1 onion, 2–3 garlic cloves, 100 g (4 oz) barley, 1 carrot, half a koshered goose breast and 2 goose feet, a small piece of koshered brisket, salt

Place a portion of the washed and soaked beans in the cholent casserole, put the kugel on the bed of beans, sprinkle with the washed barley, the cleaned and chopped carrot, the meat, garlic, and the chopped onion. Cover with water, put a lid on the dish and cook it very slowly.

Cholent III

250 g (9 oz) white beans, 100 g (4 oz) barley, 1 onion, 2–3 garlic cloves, 1 piece of koshered brisket or breast of koshered goose, salt, pepper, paprika

Soak the beans overnight. Place the kugel in the cholent casserole and cover with a small plate. Put a portion of the beans on top of the kugel, then add the brisket or goose meat and the rest of the beans. Sprinkle the top with the finely chopped onion and minced garlic. Cover with water. Season to taste and bake in the oven in a very lightly covered dish.

Kugel I

Blend together 150 g (5 oz) plain flour with 7 tablespoons goose fat, a pinch of salt, paprika and a small amount of water. Form a sausage of the mixture and place it on top of the beans and cook them together.

Kugel II

Beat a whole egg together with a pinch of salt, ground black pepper and paprika, stir in a tablespoonful of goose fat and enough flour to produce a stiff dumpling dough. Roll it out in the shape of a rectangle and place it on top of the cholent.

Kugel III

Knead together approximately 200 g (7 oz) plain flour with 2 tablespoons goose fat, a pinch of salt, ground black pepper and paprika. Stuff the mixture into a koshered goose neck. Sew up both ends of the neck and cook it in the cholent.

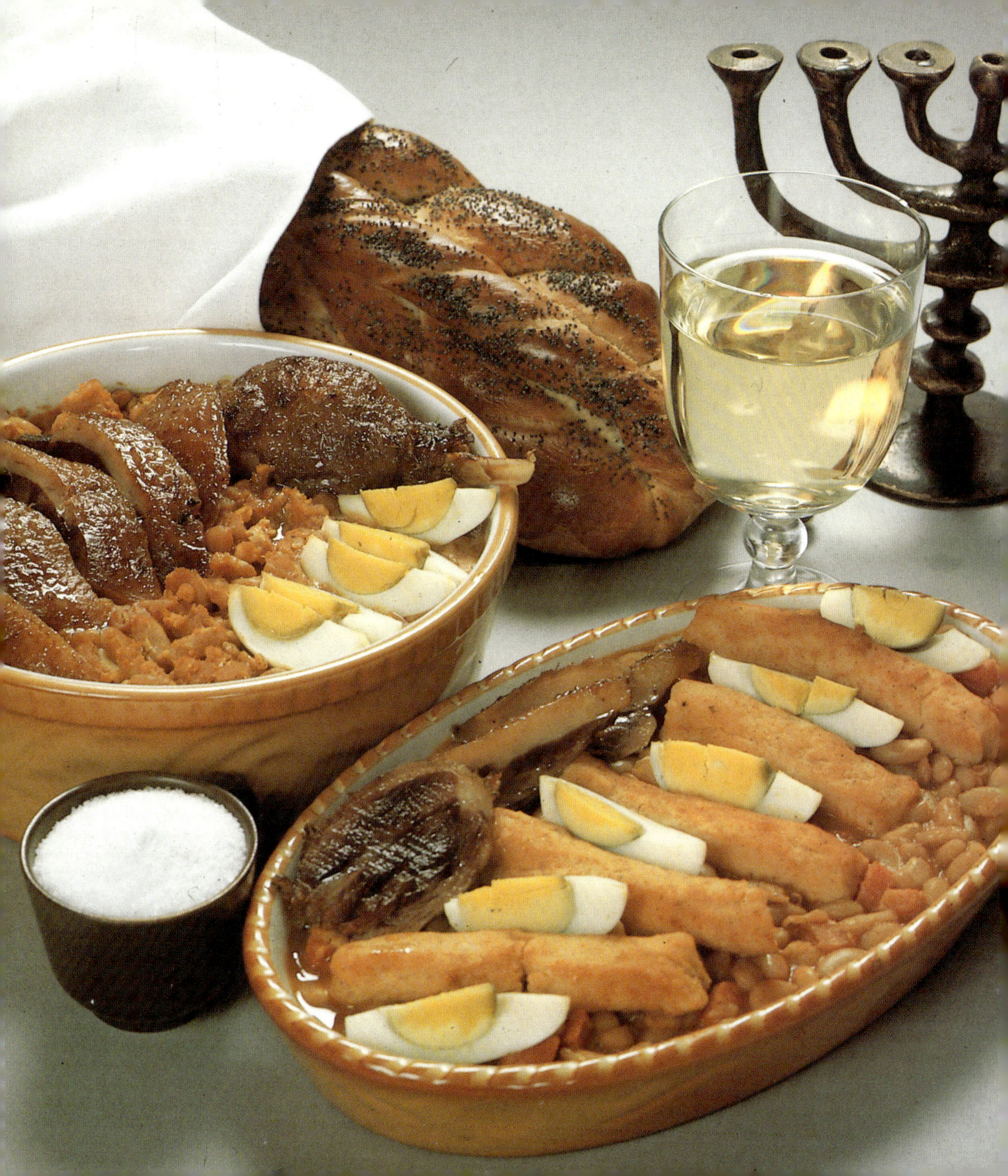

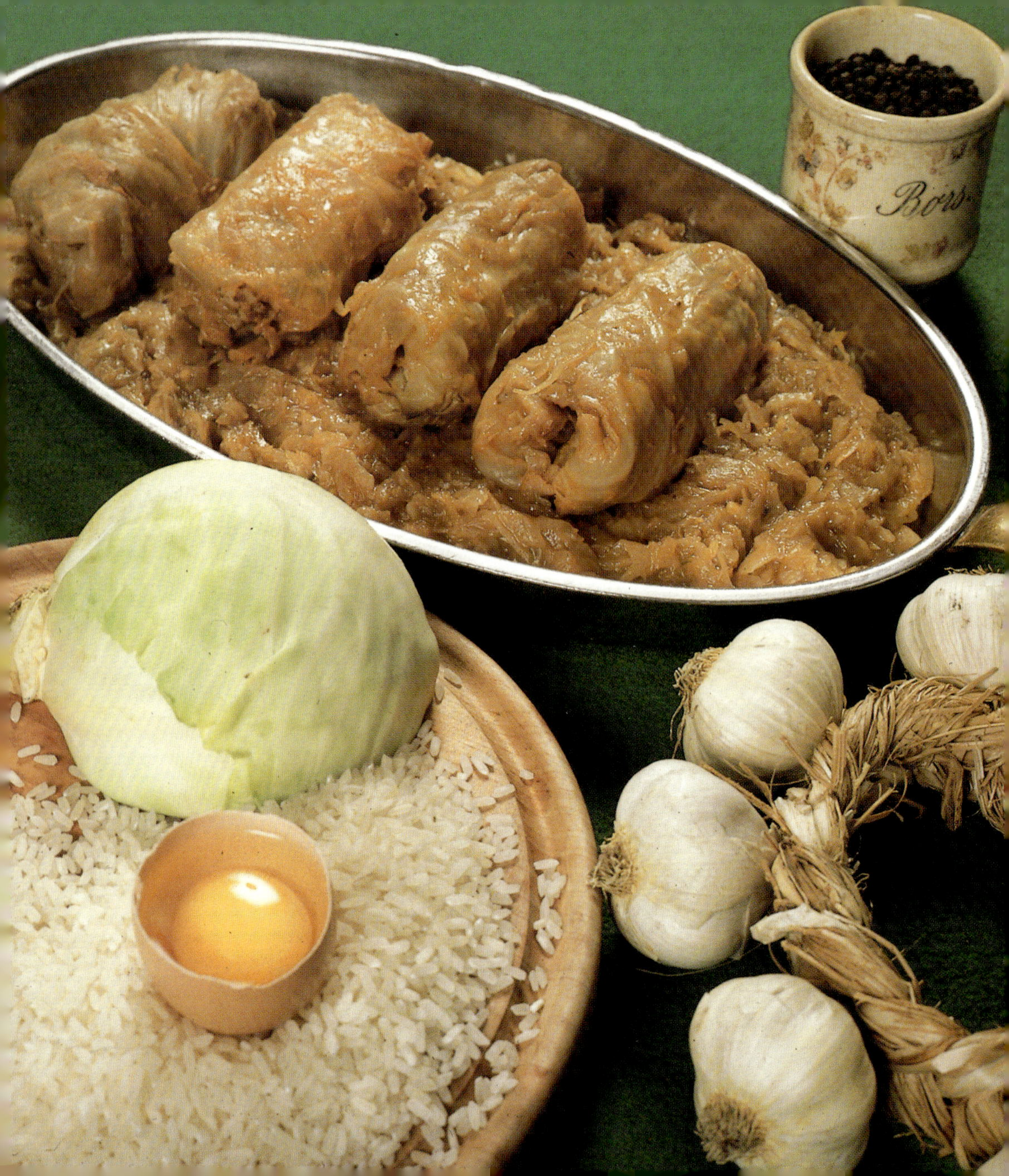
Bors

Kugel IV

Knead together approximately 150 g (5 oz) cornflour (which has been scalded and drained) with 5 tablespoons plain flour, and 2–3 tablespoons goose fat. Season with salt, pepper and sugar. Roll out the dough and place a small plate over it so that it will not run. Put the kugel on the bottom of the cholent dish and cook it together with the beans.

Kugel V

Soak a slice of challah in water, then squeeze it dry. Grate a large onion, mince 2 garlic cloves and mix them with the challah, adding some salt, pepper and paprika and enough flour to make a nice smooth dough. Form the mixture into one large dumpling and place it in the middle of the cholent.

Kugel VI

Grate 500 g (18 oz) raw potatoes. Soak 2 slices of challah in water, squeeze, then dry and mix together with the potatoes. Add enough cubed beef suet to make it juicy and season with salt and pepper. Place the mixture in an earthenware dish in the oven next to the cholent.

Peppers Stuffed with Pike

450 g (1 lb) pike, 100 g (4 oz) rice, 25 g (1 oz) butter, 1 egg, 4 fresh sweet peppers, 25 g (1 oz) butter, 1 tbs flour, 225 ml (8 fl oz) tomato juice, salt, ground black pepper

Wash and clean the pike. Discard the head, skin and innards, then carefully fillet the fish. Pound or mince the fish. Steam the rice and mix with the minced fish, then add the slightly beaten egg and half the butter. Season the mixture to taste and stir until smooth. Slice the tops off the peppers and remove the seeds and ribs. Put the peppers into a pan and pour boiling water over them. Drain the pepper and stuff them with the fish mixture. Make a roux using the second knob of butter, add the tomato juice, bring it to the boil, place the stuffed peppers into the simmering sauce and cook until tender.

Stuffed Cabbage

FISH

Jellied Fish (Gefillte Fish) I

1 kg (2 lb) fish, 3–4 onions, 2–3 garlic cloves, salt, 4–5 peppercorns, a pinch of sugar, a few drops of vinegar, 1–2 bay leaves, 1 tsp honey, 2 cloves, 50 g (2 oz) raisins

Place the cleaned fish in a baking dish, then prepare the marinade. Put the bay leaves, cloves, pepper, onions, salt, garlic, washed raisins, honey, sugar, and salt into slightly vinegary water. Bake the fish in the oven, constantly basting it with the marinade. When the fish becomes tender, remove it from the marinade, let it cool and then slice. Thicken the marinade and strain it through a cheesecloth. Pour the sauce over the fish. Leave in a cold place until it gels.

Jellied Fish (Gefillte Fish) II

1 kg (2 lb) fish, 1 parsley root (parsnip), 1 carrot, 3–4 medium-sized onions, 2–3 garlic cloves, sweet peppercorns, 1 hard-boiled egg, 2 peppers, 3 or 4 tomatoes, salt

Steam the cleaned fish, fish head, fish tail, innards, fish roe in a small amount of water. Add the cored and seeded peppers and sliced tomatoes. When the fish becomes tender, pour the liquid on top of the sliced fish. Add the onion, garlic, peppers, salt, the cleaned and sliced vegetables and cook together with the fish. Replace any water that may have evaporated. Remove the fish and thicken the liquid if needed. Slice the hard-boiled egg. Strain the thickened sauce over the fish and egg and let it gel.

Jellied Pike

1 medium-sized pike, 1 litre (1¾ pints) water, 2 tbs vinegar, 1 large onion, 1 carrot, 1 parsley root (parsnip), the grated rind of 1 lemon, 4–5 cloves, 2 bay leaves, 2–3 black peppercorns, a pinch of thyme

Place the cleaned fish on a plate. Prepare the court-bouillon: cook the peeled onions and prepared vegetables, the seasonings and the lemon rind in water. Add the fish and continue cooking very slowly. When the fish becomes tender, remove it from the court-bouillon, thicken the sauce, then pour it over the fish. Decorate the platter with vegetable slices. Let it gel.

Pike Stuffed with Walnuts

*1 kg (2 lb) pike, 2 slices of challah, 200 g (7 oz) coarsely chopped walnuts,
2 egg yolks, salt, ground black pepper*

Sprinkle the cleaned fish with salt. Soak the challah in water and squeeze it dry. Add the egg yolks, salt and pepper to the challah and mix it with the coarsely chopped walnuts. Stuff the fish cavity with the nut mixture and sew up the opening. Pre-heat the oven to 180 °C (350 °F, Gas Mark 4). Bake the fish covered with foils in a buttered or oiled dish for about 30 minutes or until cooked.

Fish with Walnuts I

*1 fish weighing approximately 1 kg (2 lb), 1 large onion, 1 tbs plain flour,
1 tbs sugar, 100 g (4 oz) of ground walnuts, 2 carrots, 1 parsley root,
225 ml (8 fl oz) sour cream, salt, ground black pepper*

Clean, slice and salt the fish. Prepare the court-bouillon: clean and slice the vegetables, slice the onions and place all vegetables together with the salt, pepper and sugar into a saucepan. Cook slowly in water. When the vegetables are half-done, add the fish and steam slowly until tender. Blend the sour cream with the flour until smooth, sprinkle with the walnuts, pour the sour cream mixture over the fish and simmer until it boils.

Fish with Walnuts II

*1 fish weighing approximately 1 kg (2 lb), 1 large onion, 2 garlic cloves,
1 parsley root (1 parsnip), 1 carrot, 1 tbs plain flour, 1 tbs ground almonds,
50 g (2 oz) of walnuts, salt*

Salt and slice the cleaned fish. Cook the peeled onions and the prepared vegetables in water until they are half-done and then add the fish slices. When the fish is tender, mix the minced garlic with the flour, almonds, and walnuts and, adding small amounts of water, work into a smooth paste. Remove the fish from the cooking water, strain the liquid through a cheesecloth, add the paste and bring to the boil. Finally, return the fish to the sauce.

Fish with Walnuts III

1–1½ kg (2–2½ lb) pike, salt, 1 small celeriac, 1 small carrot, 1 small parsley root (parsnip), 2–3 lumps of sugar, 100 g (4 oz) ground walnuts, 3 tbs plain flour, 1 tsp goose fat

Clean the pike. Grate the cleaned vegetables and season them with salt. Cook the vegetables in water until tender, then add the fish and continue cooking. Brown the lumps of sugar in the goose fat and stir in the walnuts, sprinkle flour over the mixture, taking care not to burn it. Work it into a smooth paste, adding small amounts of water. Gently stir pellets of the paste into the broth and bring it to simmering point.

Fish Polonaise (Carpe à la Juive)

1 kg (2 lb) fish, 1 glass of kosher sweet red wine, 225 ml (8 fl oz) sour cream, 1 tbs plain flour, 50 g (2 oz) raisins, 50 g (2 oz) almonds, sugar, salt

Fillet the cleaned fish, and place into a buttered fish steamer, pour a glass of sweet red wine over it and steam until tender.
Place the steamed fish on a platter. Blend the sour cream with the flour, washed and soaked raisins, the blanched and slivered almonds, a little sugar, a pinch of pepper and salt and simmer together with the fish broth. Pour the sauce over the fish and serve.

Pike with Sour Cream

1 kg (2 lb) pike, 225 ml (8 fl oz) sour cream, 1 tbs plain flour, vinegar, sugar, salt

Steam the fish in slightly vinegary water in a steamer. Remove the fish and place it on a platter. Blend the fish broth with the sour cream, flour, salt and sugar and bring to the boil. Pour the sauce over the fish and serve.

Serbian Fish

1 kg (2 lb) fish, 2–3 garlic cloves, a pinch of ground black pepper, salt, 3 onions, 6–7 small red-skinned potatoes, butter, sour cream, sweet pepper, tomatoes

Rub the cleaned fish with garlic, pepper and salt and leave to rest. Butter a baking dish. First spread a layer of boiled, peeled and sliced potatoes in the pan, cover it with sliced onions and salt. Place the fish on the bed of potatoes and onions. Score the fish and put slices of sweet pepper and tomato into the incisions. Baste the fish with sour cream and butter, and bake it in the oven.

Sweet-and-Sour Fish

1 kg (2 lb) fish, 50 g (2 oz) raisins, 2–3 tsp ground almonds, 1 tsp grated lemon rind, 2–3 cloves, a few drops of vinegar, 1 tsp sugar

Place the cleaned fish in a pan. Prepare the court-bouillon: boil enough water to cover the fish with a few drops of vinegar, salt, lemon rind, cloves and almonds. Pour the liquid over the fish and poach until tender.

Gefillte Helzel I
for Friday night

about 1 kg (2 lb) pike, 2 slices of challah, 1 egg, 2 onions, 2 parsley roots (parsnips), 1 carrot, 2 garlic cloves, salt, ground black pepper

Clean the fish well, removing the gut and the gills. With a sharp knife make a slit around the neck and separate the skin from the flesh without tearing; then fillet the fish and mince it. Mix the minced fish with the *challah* that has been soaked and squeezed dry. Add the eggs, salt, pepper, and grated onions. Stuff this mixture under the skin of the fish.

The *aspic* is prepared in the following way: cook the cleaned vegetables and the onion in salted water, together with the fish head and backbone. Strain the liquid over the fish and continue to cook it very slowly. Remove the fish and place on a platter, pour the liquid over it and let it gel.

Gefillte Helzel II

about 1 kg (2 lb) pike, 2 eggs, 2 tbs challah crumbs, 2 tbs oil, 1 small and 1 large onion, 1 parsley root (parsnip), 1 carrot, salt, ground black pepper and, in the summer, some sweet peppers

Clean the fish and proceed with removing the skin as in the recipe above.
For the filling: blend the crumbs with the grated small onion, the eggs, oil, salt and pepper and stuff it under the skin of the fish. The aspic is prepared as above. Pour the liquid over the fish, but serve the fish together with its head. Let the liquid gel.

Stuffed Pike I

1 medium-sized pike, 1 large onion, 2 garlic cloves, the grated rind of 2 lemons, 1 slice of soaked challah, 4 eggs, ground black pepper, nutmeg, salt, water

After cleaning the fish, remove the skin. Mince the fish that has been removed from the bones. Put the minced fish into a large bowl and add the minced onions, the garlic, eggs, the soaked and squeezed challah, the seasonings and blend well. Stuff the mixture back into the fish skin and brush with beaten egg yolk. Fry it in butter, adding very little water. In the olden days they used to sprinkle some oil of bay leaf on top.

Stuffed Pike II

about 1 kg (2 lb) pike, 1 slice of challah, 200 g (7 oz) walnuts, 2 eggs, pinch of marjoram, salt

Clean the pike. Separate the eggs. Whisk the egg yolks with the salt, ground walnuts and marjoram. Blend in the slice of challah that has been soaked and squeezed dry. Finally add the stiffly whipped egg whites. Stuff the filling into the fish, sew up the ends or fasten with a meat skewer. Fry in butter adding a small amount of water.

MEAT DISHES

Braised Brisket

1 kg (2 lb) koshered brisket, 6 tbs goose fat, 4–5 garlic cloves, salt, pinch of ground black pepper, 225 ml (8 fl oz) water, 2 large onions

Place the cleaned brisket in a well-greased, ovenproof dish or pan, then sprinkle with the finely chopped onions, the minced garlic, salt and seasoning. Pour over the water, cover with a well-fitting lid and bake slowly in a pre-heated oven at 160 °C (325 °F, Gas Mark 3) for about 2 hours until tender.

Ox-Tongue in Raisin Sauce

1 large koshered ox-tongue, 1 large onion, 5–6 blanched almonds, 10–15 raisins, 2 tbs goose fat or oil, 1 tsp sugar, 1 tbs plain flour, 1 parsley root (parsnip), 1 carrot, salt, 4–5 peppercorns

Pour boiling water over the tongue; if it is very tough, cook it for a while, then remove the skin. Place the tongue in water together with the cleaned vegetables, pepper and salt, and cook until tender. Mash the vegetables together with the almonds and raisins. Dice the onions and brown in the goose fat. After sweating the onions, add the sugar and continue to brown. When the onions are slightly pinkish, sprinkle in the flour and pour it over the mashed vegetables, raisins, and almonds. Add a little water, bring to the boil and pour the sauce over the tongue.

Golden Vegetable Pot Roast

1 kg (2 lb) koshered brisket, salt, pinch of ground black pepper, rind of half a lemon, a small handful of raisins, a pinch of cinnamon, 1 large onion, 1 tbs honey

Put the brisket into a pan and pour on enough water to cover. Sprinkle with salt and the black pepper. Bake in covered pan at 160 °C (325 °F, Gas Mark 3) for about 2 hours. When the meat is half-done, add the lemon rind, the washed and soaked raisins, cinnamon and the diced onion. Add the honey before the meat is completely done.

Braised Beef

1 kg (2 lb) koshered rib of beef, 6–7 tbs goose fat, 1 large onion, 2–3 garlic cloves, 1 carrot, 1 parsley root (parsnip), a pinch of paprika, salt, a pinch of ground black pepper, flour as needed

Brown the meat on both sides in the hot fat. Remove the meat and place on a platter. Place the finely chopped onions and sliced vegetables into the same fat. Season with salt and pepper and cook until soft and golden. Put the meat back into the pan and cook in the oven at 160 °C (325°F, Gas Mark 3) for about 2 hours, replacing any liquid that might have evaporated. Remove the meat, purée the vegetables and place the meat back together with the puréed vegetables and sauce. If the sauce is too thin, thicken it with a little flour.

Mock Fish I

1 large breast of koshered chicken or koshered boiling fowl, 1 slice of challah, 2 garlic cloves, 1 small onion, a pinch of ground black pepper, 1 egg, salt
For the cooking liquid: 1 parsley root (parsnip), 1 carrot, 1 medium-sized onion, 1 small celeriac, salt, ½ litre (¾ pint) water

Bone the chicken and mince the meat. Soak and squeeze dry the challah and mix with the minced chicken. Add the egg, salt, pepper, the minced garlic and the finely chopped onion. Wet your hands and form small balls of the mixture.

Cook the sliced vegetables and onion in water. When the vegetables are half-done, carefully add the meatballs and simmer. Place the meatballs and vegetables on a platter and let it gel in a cool place.

Stuffed Turkey Neck

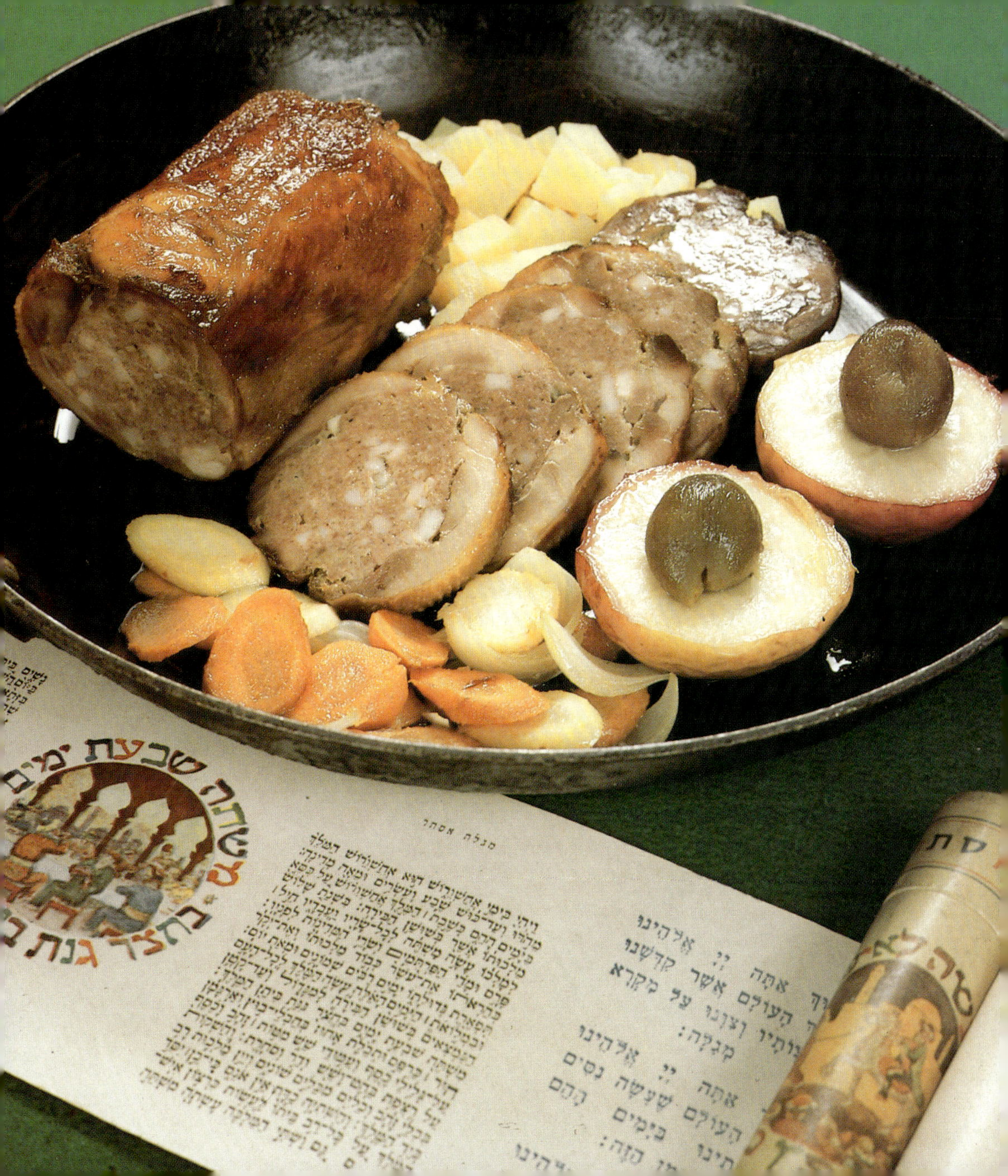

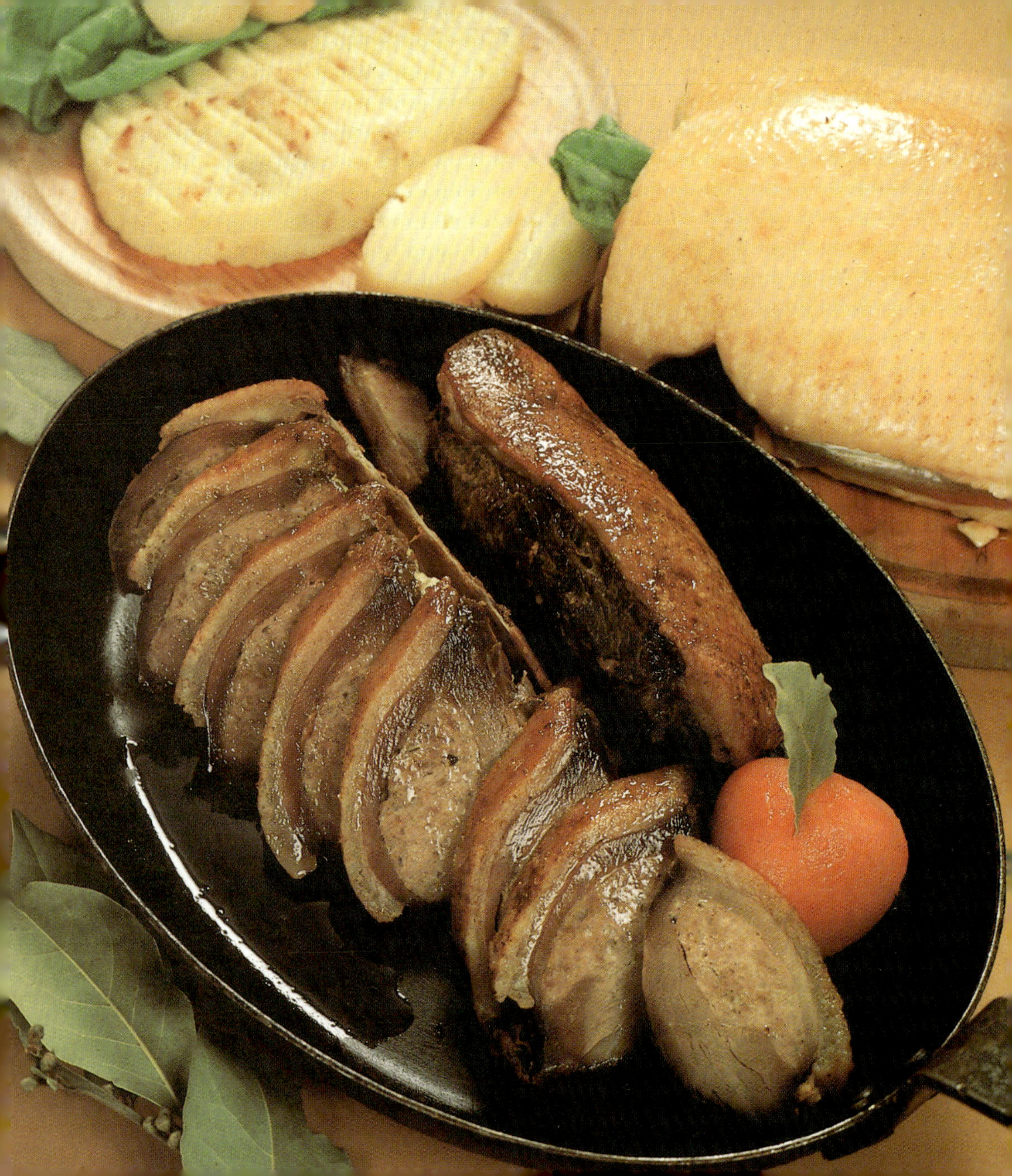

Mock Fish II

*200–300 g (7–11 oz) koshered minced veal, 1 slice of challah, 1 egg,
a pinch of pepper, a small onion, 2–3 garlic cloves, a pinch of paprika, salt
For the cooking liquid: 1 small carrot, 1 small parsley root (parsnip),
1 large onion, salt, a pinch of ground pepper, 1 large garlic clove,
½ litre (¾ pint) water*

Mix the veal with the challah which has been soaked and squeezed dry. Add the egg, salt, pepper, grated onion and the minced garlic and stir thoroughly until blended. Form small balls from the mixture using wet hands.

Prepare the *cooking liquid:* simmer together the sliced vegetables, salt, onion, garlic and pepper in a saucepan. When the vegetables are half-done, drop the meatballs into the liquid.

Lift the cooked meatballs onto a platter and strain the juice over them. Decorate the platter with the steamed vegetables. Let it gel. The meatballs may also be decorated with sautéed onions.

Meat Kugel

*500 g (18 oz) koshered and minced chuck steak, 3 slices of challah,
2–3 tbs goose fat, salt, pepper, paprika, juice and grated rind of half a lemon,
4 eggs, 2 bay leaves, a few peppercorns, 7–10 tbs goose fat for baking*

Mix the minced steak thoroughly with the slices of challah which have been soaked and squeezed dry. Mix in the egg, lemon, seasonings and goose fat. Put the bay leaves, peppercorns and the meat-mixture shaped into a loaf in a shallow baking dish or tin, with 7 cm (3 inches) of water. Bake in a moderate oven at 180 °C (350 °F, Gas Mark 4) for 1–1 ¼ hours, until cooked.

Stuffed Turkey Neck (Gefillte Helzel) I

*1 koshered turkey neck and wings, 1 breast of koshered turkey, 2–3 garlic
cloves, salt, a pinch of pepper, 1 egg, 1 slice of challah, 2 hard-boiled eggs,
1 large onion, a pinch of paprika, 3 tbs goose fat*

Keep the turkey neck intact. Remove the breast from the bone and mince or chop finely. Mix well with the soaked and squeezed challah, the raw egg, salt, pepper, paprika, the finely chopped onion

Stuffed Breast of Goose

and the minced garlic. Fill the neck cavity with this mixture, placing the boiled eggs in the middle. Sew up both ends of the neck with a needle and strong thread. Boil the neck in a small amount of water, then brown, basting frequently with hot goose fat until golden.

Stuffed Turkey Neck (Gefillte Helzel) II

1 koshered turkey neck and wings, 1 breast of koshered turkey, 2 slices of challah, 1 koshered turkey liver, 1 small onion, a pinch of ground black pepper, salt, a pinch of paprika, 2 hard-boiled eggs, 2 tbs semolina, 2 eggs, 4–5 tbs goose fat, 225 ml (8 fl oz) water

Remove the breast from the bone and mince or chop finely. Scrape the liver and brown it together with the braised onion. Chop the eggs and mix them with the soaked and squeezed challah. Stir in the liver and onions, eggs, minced turkey, pepper, salt, paprika, semolina and the raw egg. Fill the skin of the turkey neck with this mixture, sew up the ends with a needle and thread. Boil the neck in a small amount of water, basting frequently with hot goose fat until golden brown.

Stuffed Turkey Neck (Gefillte Helzel) III
for Passover

the neck of a koshered turkey cock, a small amount of turkey meat, matzo, matzo meal, 1 tbs goose fat, salt, a pinch of pepper, 1 raw egg, 1 boiled egg

Remove the skin from the turkey neck along with a small amount of neck meat. Mince, blend or finely chop the turkey meat, add to it the soaked and squeezed matzo and enough matzo meal to make an easily handled mixture. Fill the skin of the neck with this mixture and the whole boiled egg. Steam the neck in a small amount of water, basting frequently with hot goose fat until golden brown.

Stuffed Breast of Goose

1 large koshered breast of goose, the skin of koshered goose neck, 1 small slice of challah, salt, pepper, 2–3 garlic cloves, 1 egg, 2–3 tbs goose fat

Bone the goose breast. Mince the meat and mix it together with the soaked and squeezed challah, the pressed or chopped garlic, egg, and seasoning.

Stuff the goose skin with this mixture and tie up both ends. Steam the stuffed neck in a small amount of water and goose fat, let all the water evaporate and sauté until brown.

Stuffed Goose Neck

1 koshered goose neck (skin only), 50–60 g (2–3 oz) koshered goose meat, 50–60 g (2–3 oz) koshered turkey meat, 2 large boiled potatoes, 1 large onion, salt, ground black pepper, 3 tbs goose fat

Tie one end of the goose neck skin. Mix the minced goose and turkey meat with the chopped onion, mashed potatoes, salt and pepper and fill the neck with the stuffing mixture. Steam the stuffed neck in a small amount of water and goose fat and let it brown.

Goose Sausage with Lungs

1 koshered goose crop, 500 g (18 oz) koshered calf's lungs, 50 g (2 oz) rice, 1 egg, 1 garlic clove, 3 tbs goose fat, ground black pepper, salt

Carefully clean the crop, leaving the skin intact and using the part that connects with the gizzard. Cook the calf's lungs in salted water and mince them finely. Cook the rice and mix with the minced lungs, egg, the pressed or finely chopped garlic, salt and pepper. Stuff the mixture into the crop, sew up the ends, and steam with the goose fat in a small amount of water until all the water evaporates and the crop is browned.

Galantine of Goose (Jellied Goose) I

koshered giblets of a large goose, 1 parsley root (parsnip), 1 carrot, 1 small celeriac, salt, 4–5 black peppercorns, 1 large onion, 1–2 garlic cloves

Cook the giblets together with the sliced vegetables, salt, pepper and onions in 450 ml (¾ pint) water. Simmer until the meat falls away from the bones. Remove the bones, place the goose meat on a dish and cover with the strained liquid. Set aside in a cold place until the jelly has set and serve.

Galantine of Goose (Jellied Goose) II

*koshered goose giblets, 2 large onions, 2–3 garlic cloves, 5–6 peppercorns,
a pinch of paprika*

Cook the giblets together with the salt, pepper, onions and a clove of garlic. When the meat is tender, remove the bones. Press the rest of the garlic and spread it on the goose meat. Sprinkle the meat with paprika. Strain the liquid through a cheesecloth and pour it over the meat. Refrigerate until set and serve.

Roast Leg of Goose I

*1 koshered goose leg, 4–5 garlic cloves, a small piece of unrendered goose fat,
salt, pepper, 5–6 tbs goose fat, 1 tsp paprika, 1 large onion,
450 ml (¾ pint) water*

Make slits on the thick parts of the goose leg; put slivers of the peeled garlic, salt and pepper into the slits, also insert small pieces of the goose fat. Roll the pieces in paprika and place them in a pan well-greased with goose fat. Put the sliced onion in the bottom of the pan and pour the water over it. Braise the meat slowly at 160 °C (325 °F, Gas Mark 3), basting frequently, until tender.

Roast Leg of Goose II

*1 koshered goose leg, 5–6 tbs goose fat, 4–5 garlic cloves, 1 large onion, salt,
a pinch of pepper, 750 ml (1¼ pints) water*

Make slits on the thick part of the goose leg, put slivers of the peeled garlic, salt and pepper into the slits.
Finely mince the onion and brown in goose fat. Place the leg on top of the browned onion. Add a little water and baste with the juices. Bake slowly at 160 °C (325 °F, Gas Mark 3) until tender. Breast of goose is prepared in the same way.

Fried Goose Liver

*1 medium-sized goose liver, unrendered goose fat, 1 garlic clove,
1 medium-sized onion*

Sear the liver on both sides over glowing embers or in a very heavy pan, to kosher it. Place it, together with the goose fat and any fat remaining on the liver, in a pan covered with water. Add to the liquid the clove of garlic and the sliced onion. Simmer together, then let all the water evaporate so that the liver is browned.

Fried Goose or Duck Liver

1 liver, 1 onion, 2–3 tbs goose fat

Sear the liver on both sides over glowing embers to kosher it. Slice the onion and sauté it in goose fat. Place the liver on the onions and cover it with water. When the liver is tender, let all the water evaporate so that the liver is browned.

Liver Dumplings

1 small goose or duck liver, 1 small slice of challah, 1 egg, a pinch of ground black pepper, 1 small onion, 2 garlic cloves, 10 tbs goose fat for frying

Sear the liver on both sides to kosher it. Scrape the liver with a sharp knife. Mix the scraped liver with the egg, the soaked and squeezed challah, the grated onion, the pressed garlic and pepper. Blend thoroughly. Form into small balls, flatten their tops and fry in hot goose fat.

Stuffed Casings

koshered beef or veal casings, proportionate amounts of potatoes, plain flour, onions, ground black pepper, salt

Clean the casings thoroughly inside and out. Grate as many potatoes as needed to fill the casings without filling the cavity too tightly. Grate the onions into the potato mixture, season with salt and pepper and add enough flour to make a moist mixture. Fill the casings, turned inside out, if preferred, with the stuffing, then tie both ends with kitchen string. Steam using a little water with goose fat added and finally brown on both sides. Of course, if you make it for Passover, omit the flour and use matzo meal or potato flour instead.

Lung with Garlic

1 large koshered calf's lung, 4–5 tbs goose fat, an equal amount of plain flour, 3 large garlic cloves, salt, ground black pepper

Soak the lung in salted water before mincing it. Make a light roux of the goose fat and flour and add the pressed garlic. Slowly add the liquid in which the lung was cooked, and then the minced lung. Bring to the boil and simmer until thickened. Serve with potatoes.

PERISHABLE STUFFINGS

Lung Sausage (Lingenwurst or Lüngenwurst) I

koshered beef or veal casings, 1 kg (2 lb) lung, 200 g (7 oz) rice, 2–3 eggs, 4–5 tbs goose or duck fat, 5–6 garlic cloves, ground black pepper, salt

Scrape the casings, washed and turned inside out, repeating the procedure until they are completely clean. Steam the beef lung in salted water until half-cooked. Remove from the water and mince. Boil the rice. Mix together the minced lung, cooked rice, eggs, goose or duck fat, pressed garlic, salt and pepper.
Stuff this mixture into the casings using a sausage-filler. Form small or large sausages according to taste and tie up both ends of the sausages. Place the sausages back into the liquid in which the lung was cooked and steam for a short time. Remove from the liquid and store in a refrigerator. Fry the lung sausages on both sides in hot fat and serve.

Lung Sausage (Lüngenwurst) II

500 g (18 oz) koshered calf's lung, 1 large onion, 2 garlic cloves, 1 tbs plain flour, 2 tbs goose fat, salt, a pinch of pepper, a pinch of marjoram, calf's casings, goose fat for frying

Cook the calf's lung in salted water, then mince. Sauté the diced onion and garlic in goose fat, and sprinkle with salt, pepper, marjoram and flour. Add only a small amount of water, so that the mixture will not become runny. Stir until all lumps disappear. Fill the casings with the mixture. Sew up both ends of the casings or close with a skewer. Grease the pan with goose fat, add a little water, place the casings in the pan and simmer until tender. Finally, allow the sausage to brown.

Liver Sausage

500 g (18 oz) koshered calf's liver, 3 eggs, salt, 1 tsp ground black pepper, marjoram according to taste, koshered casings, 5–6 tbs goose fat

Sear the liver on both sides over glowing embers, mince it, then season with salt, pepper and marjoram. Blend in the eggs and 1–2 tablespoons of goose fat.
Prepare the casings according to the recipe for lung sausage. Fill the casings with the mixture, steam using a small amount of water, then brown on both sides.

Pcha (Calf's-Foot Jelly)

2 koshered calves' feet, 2 slices of challah, 2 large garlic cloves, salt

Cook the calves' feet in a litre (1¾ pints) of water. When the meat separates from the bones, lift the feet out of the water and remove the bones. Cut the challah slices in half, toast them and spread with pressed garlic. Place a piece of challah into each of four individual soup bowls, strain the bouillon over it and finally add the meat. Serve very hot.

Veal Krezli

Calf's casings, 500 g (18 oz) koshered veal, salt, ground black pepper, 3–4 garlic cloves, caraway seeds

Mince the veal and season with salt, pepper, marjoram, caraway seeds and pressed garlic. Stuff this mixture into the casings (see Lung Sausages). Steam using a small amount of water, then brown on both sides.

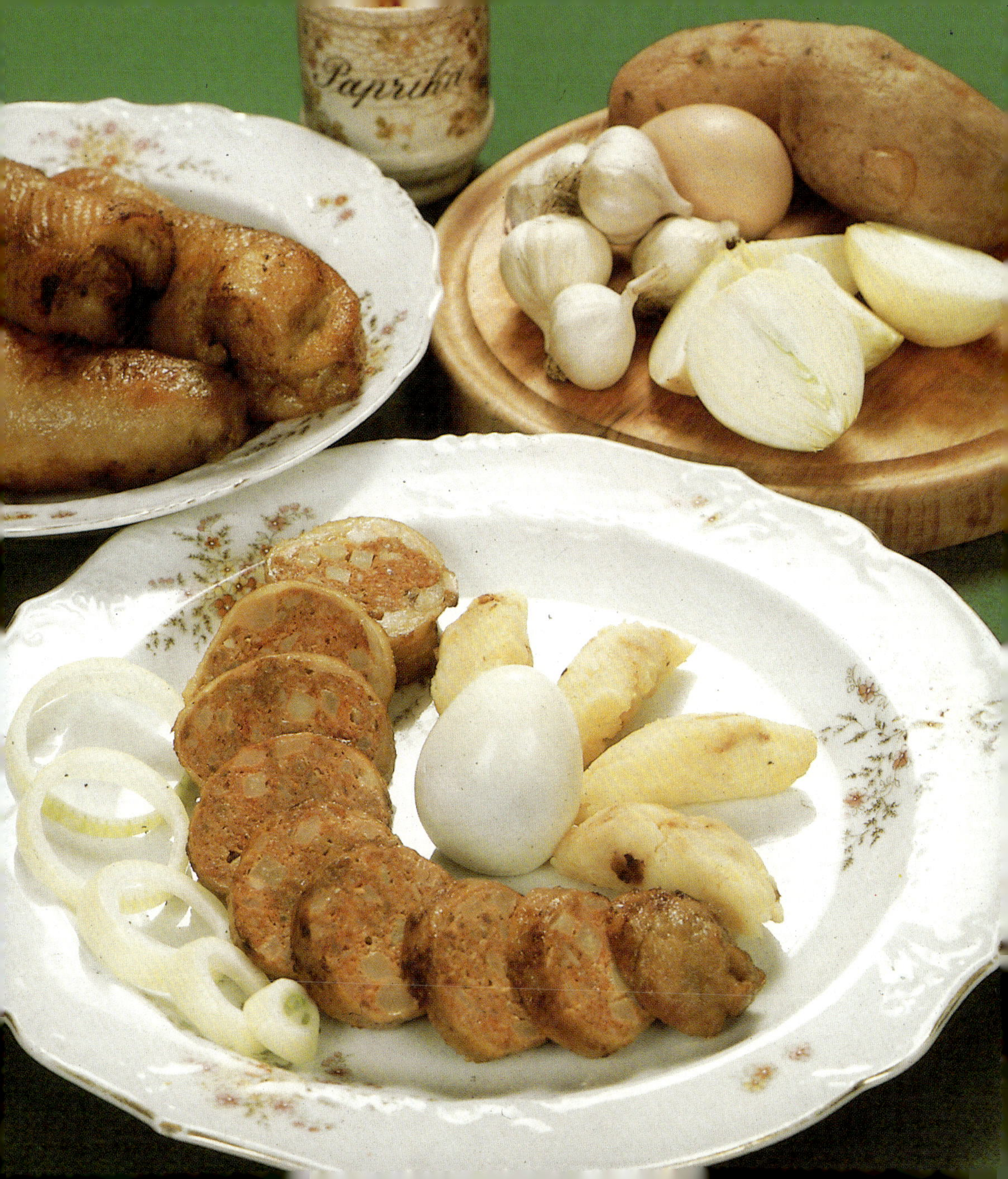
Paprika

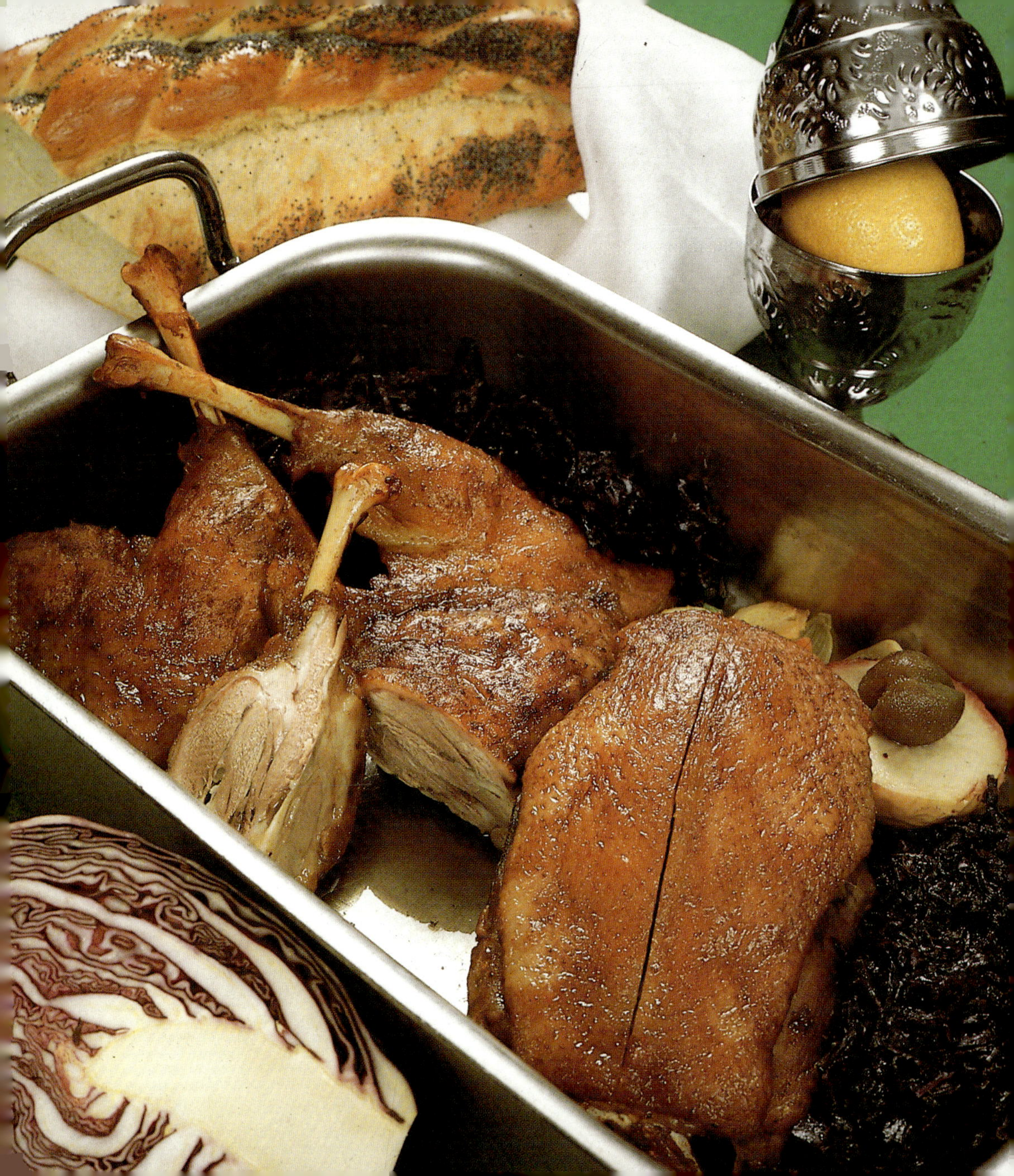

TASTY TIDBITS

Egg and Onion Spread (Eier Ziebel) I
for the Sabbath

1–2 hard-boiled eggs per person, 1 large onion, goose fat, salt

Chop the hard-boiled eggs, then mash them using a fork and mix together with enough goose fat to make a light spread. Chop a large onion and stir it into the eggs. If there is any left-over goose or duck liver, it may be added to the mixture.

Egg and Onion Spread (Eier Zibel) II

*2–3 hard-boiled eggs per person, 1 large onion, goose or duck fat,
1 medium-sized boiled potato, salt, paprika*

Peel and grate the eggs. Add enough fat to make them moist, add a large grated onion, the grated boiled potato and blend well. Season with salt and paprika.

Inarsz (Leaf Fat, Mock Bacon)

Remove the fat from the underbelly of the goose and kosher it. Spread it evenly with minced garlic, sprinkle with paprika and cool it in the refrigerator.

Mock Calf's-Head Cheese

30–40 cm (8–12 in) koshered, cleaned casings of veal, ½ koshered turkey breast, 50–100 g (2–4 oz) koshered veal or beef, 1 koshered calf's foot (the fore-foot), 1 small calf's ear, 100–150 g (4–5 oz) koshered smoked ox-tongue, the same amount of koshered goose, plain flour, 5–6 garlic cloves,

Roast Leg of Goose

a pinch of paprika, 7–8 peppercorns, 2 juniper berries, a few coriander seeds, salt, ground black pepper

Cut the turkey breast, the calf's foot and ear into chunks and boil in water. Remove all the scum which has accumulated during cooking. Add the salt, paprika, peppercorns, juniper, and coriander. When the meat is done, remove it from the liquid and cut it into long strips. Cut the smoked tongue into long pieces too. Sprinkle all the meat with flour, add the pressed garlic and add more salt, pepper and paprika if required. Blend thoroughly and fill the casings with this mixture. (For the method of preparation, see the Veal Sausage recipe.) Tie both ends with string and put the sausage back into the cooking liquid, steam for about half an hour, then remove and place the sausage between two boards and weigh it down. Leave it for a day. Tie the boards with string and smoke the sausage. Refrigerate and serve thinly sliced.

KUGELS AND NOODLES

Apple Kugel

*2–3 apples, 1 slice of challah, 50 g (2 oz) walnuts, 50 g (2 oz) raisins,
2 tbs sugar, a pinch of ground cinnamon*

Wipe and grate the apples. Mix together the apples, cinnamon, sugar, walnuts and the washed and soaked raisins in a bowl. Soak the challah for 3 minutes, then squeeze out all the excess water. Add to the apple mixture and blend well. Form small balls and serve as a side dish.

Lokshen Kugel I

*500 g (18 oz) wide egg noodles (home-made or shop-bought fresh paste),
4 egg yolks, 50 g (2 oz) butter, sugar*

Knead a nice, firm egg-noodle dough, cut it into wide strips and drop them into boiling water. Drain well. Meanwhile butter a deep casserole. Mix the drained noodles with the egg yolks and put them into the casserole. Sprinkle with sugar and serve immediately.

Lokshen Kugel II

*500 g (18 oz) wide egg noodles, 6–8 egg yolks, 50 g (2 oz) butter,
a handful of raisins, the grated rind of 1 lemon, a few tbs of honey*

Cook the home-made or fresh commercial noodles. Drain well, mix with the egg yolks and place half the noodles in a buttered casserole. Put the washed and soaked raisins on top, sprinkle with grated lemon rind, sugar and honey, and cover with the rest of the noodles. Heat in the oven and serve immediately.

Note! If these pastries are to be served with a meatless meal, you can use butter instead of margarine. Always use kosher or vegetarian margarine!

PASTRIES

Gingerbread I
for Purim

2 eggs, 450 g (1 lb) sugar, 100 g (4 oz) plain flour, 3–4 tsp ground ginger, 50 g (2 oz) margarine

Break the eggs into a deep bowl. Add the sugar, ginger and melted margarine and mix well. Keep adding flour as needed to get a nice firm dough. Roll out on a smooth surface and cut out rounds using 5 cm (2 in) plain cutter. Place the rounds on a well-greased and floured baking sheet and bake until golden.
Note! The gingerbread should not be eaten on the day on which it is made as it will be too hard.

Gingerbread II

250 g (9 oz) sugar, 4 egg yolks, 1 whole egg, 250 g (9 oz) plain flour, 1 tsp powdered ginger, margarine for greasing

Whisk together the egg yolks, sugar, whole egg, powdered ginger, and work in the flour. Blend well and roll out on a flat surface, but not too thinly. Cut out rounds using a 5 cm (2 in) plain cutter. Place the rounds on a well-greased and floured baking sheet and bake until golden.

Feferkuchen (Spice Cake)

500 g (18 oz) plain flour, 2 tbs goose fat, 2 eggs, 1 tsp ground black pepper, 1 tsp salt

Knead the lightly beaten eggs together with the salt, flour, pepper and goose fat. Knead until you get a firm dough, then shape into a long roll. Place on a well-greased baking sheet and bake until golden.

Eierkuchen (Ejerkuhni, Ejerkichli) I
a Sabbath morning dish

500 g (18 oz) plain flour, a pinch of bicarbonate of soda, 4 eggs, 15 g (½ oz) margarine, a pinch of salt, soda water as needed

Mix together the bicarbonate of soda, flour, eggs, salt and margarine until you get a nice soft dough. If the dough is too firm, add a little soda water. Roll out 1 cm (½ in) thick on a lightly floured board. Transfer to a greased and floured baking sheet and bake until golden.

Eierkuchen II

500 g (18 oz) plain flour, a pinch of baking powder, 4 eggs, 2 tbs sugar, 1 tsp margarine

Mix together the baking powder, flour, eggs and margarine. Roll out the dough and transfer it to a greased and floured baking sheet and bake until golden.

Eierkuchen III

500 g (18 oz) plain flour, 4 eggs, 1 tsp margarine, a dash of kosher (sweet red) wine, a pinch of ground black pepper, a pinch of salt

Mix together the flour, margarine, pepper, salt and eggs, add the wine and roll out the dough about ⅓ cm (⅛ in) thick. Transfer to a greased baking sheet and make small cuts on top, using a sharp knife. Bake until golden.

Kugel

200 g (7 oz) floury potatoes, 5 eggs, 1–1 ½ tsp salt, 1 tsp paprika, 5 tbs goose fat, ground black pepper

Mix the peeled and grated potatoes, eggs, salt, paprika, a pinch of ground black pepper, and the goose fat. Work into a smooth dough. Roll out and transfer to a well-greased baking tin and bake slowly. Let the kugel cool, then cut into small slices and serve.

Potato Cake
for Passover

5–6 large floury boiled potatoes, 3 large raw potatoes, 2 eggs, salt, ground black pepper, 2 tbs matzo meal, margarine or goose fat

Mash the peeled boiled potatoes and mix with the grated raw potatoes, egg yolks, seasoning and the matzo meal. Knead gently until smooth, then fold in the stiffly beaten egg whites. Flatten the dough into a round shape, then transfer to a well greased baking tin (grease it either with margarine or goose fat, depending on whether it will be served with a meat or milk dish). Bake slowly.

Lekach (Honey and Spice Cake)
for the Jewish New Year

500 g (18 oz) plain flour, 500 g (18 oz) sugar, 4 tbs honey, 8 tbs oil, 4 eggs, 1 tsp bicarbonate of soda, 50 g (2 oz) raisins, 50 g (2 oz) walnuts

Brown the sugar until it is golden, taking care not to burn it. Add the honey, oil, and flour. Beat well together until smooth. Add the egg yolks, the bicarbonate of soda, and the washed and soaked raisins. Finally fold in the stiffly beaten egg whites. Transfer to a well-greased baking sheet and smooth the top to make even. Sprinkle with the walnuts and bake slowly until golden.

Teiglach (Honey Bubbles)

100 g (4 oz) plain flour, 4 eggs, 4 tbs oil, 2 tbs honey, 1 tsp bicarbonate of soda, a pinch of salt, a pinch of nutmeg, a pinch of ginger, a dash of kosher (sweet red) wine

Mix together the egg yolks, flour, oil, and honey. Add the wine, bicarbonate of soda, salt, nutmeg and ginger. Beat well together until smooth. Finally gently fold in the stiffly beaten egg whites. Pour the batter onto a well-buttered baking sheet and bake until golden.

Kranzli

4 egg yolks, 250 g (9 oz) icing sugar, 1 tsp lemon juice, 250 g (9 oz) margarine, 250 g (9 oz) plain flour, 10–15 lumps of sugar, crushed, 1 egg white

Mix together the egg yolks, flour and margarine; add the lemon juice and sugar. Knead until a firm dough is formed. Roll it out thinly into a round shape. Cut out small rounds using a 5 cm (2 in) plain cutter, then brush the tops of the rounds with the stiffly beaten egg whites. Transfer to a greased baking sheet, sprinkle crushed sugar lumps on top and bake slowly in a moderate oven. You may also wash the tops with the egg whites after the kranzli have been baking for a while, and sprinkle the crushed sugar lumps on top.

Schmaltzbaigli (Schmelzbeigel)
for Purim

8 eggs, equal weight of plain flour, a little sugar, chicken fat

Knead the flour and eggs together, add the sugar and the chicken fat. Roll the dough into a thick round shape and bake slowly in an earthenware dish.
This cake is used as a plate for pastries at Purim. Very traditional families send each other their Purim pastries placed on this roll.

Zatterka

250 g (9 oz) corn meal, 250 g (9 oz) semolina, sufficient water to get a kneadable dough, 225 ml (8 fl oz) milk

Mix the corn meal and semolina with the water to get a stiff, but workable dough. Grate on a coarse grater. Serve immediately with warm sweetened milk.

Weisskinlach (Wine Biscuits) I

300 g (11 oz) plain flour, 150 g (5 oz) margarine, 50 g (2 oz) icing sugar, 50 g (2 oz) vanilla sugar, 2 egg yolks, 1 whole egg

Mix together the flour, icing sugar, vanilla sugar, and egg yolks, then add the whole egg and blend in the margarine. Let the dough rest in a cool place. Knead, roll out and cut with a 5 cm (2 in) biscuit cutter. Bake until golden.

Weisskinlach (Wine Biscuits) II

600 g (22 oz) plain flour, 150 g (5 oz) margarine, 5 eggs, grated rind of 1 lemon, 150 g (5 oz) icing sugar, 50 g (2 oz) vanilla sugar

Mix together the flour, sugar, margarine, lemon rind and eggs. Cool the dough for a short time, then roll out and cut out various shapes with biscuit cutters. Bake.

Mish-mash Delkli (Filled Yeast Buns)

250 g (9 oz) plain flour, 10 g (⅓ oz) yeast, 225 ml (8 fl oz) milk, 200 g (7 oz) softened butter, ½ tsp sugar, ½ tsp salt, 150 g (5 oz) curd cheese or cottage cheese, 1 tbs prune jam

Heat the milk until lukewarm and mix with the sugar and yeast. Blend in about ¾ of the flour and mix until smooth. Cover with a towel and leave for 20 minutes in a warm place. Now knead the rest of the flour with half the butter and add to the yeast mixture. Let the dough rise. Knead the dough and add the remaining butter and keep kneading blending in the butter. Roll out on a flat surface. Fold the pastry in four by taking the two outer edges and folding them to the middle, then fold in the other two sides. Allow the dough to rest for 20 minutes, then repeat the procedure described above twice more at intervals of 20 minutes. Roll out the dough and cut into small rectangles. Fill the middle of the rectangles with curd cheese (cottage cheese) and jam, then pinch the edges firmly together. Place on a baking sheet, leaving sufficient room between them as the pastries tend to expand. Bake at 225 °C (435 °F, Gas Mark 7) for about 7 minutes.

Fried Goose Liver

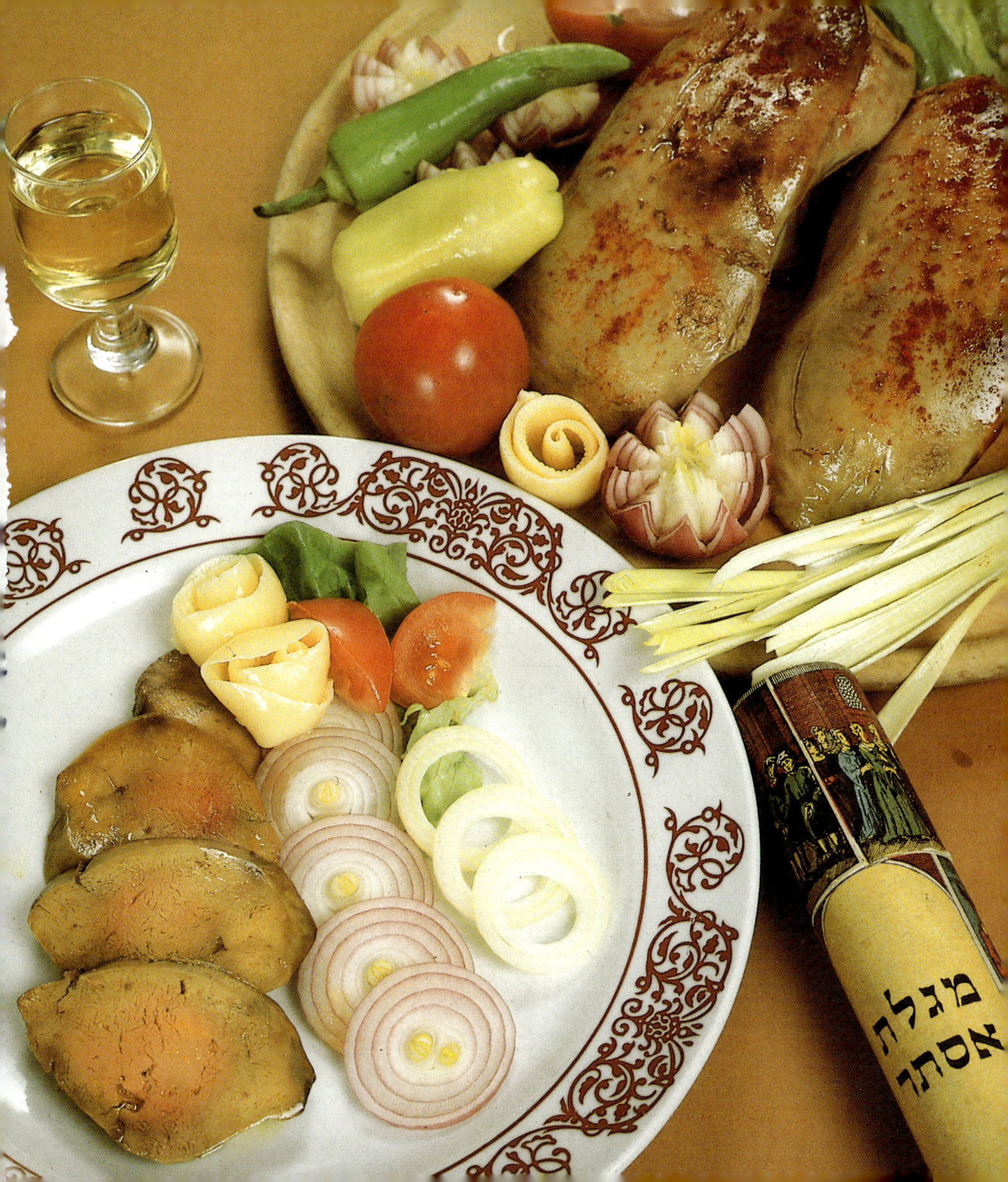
מגלת
אסתר

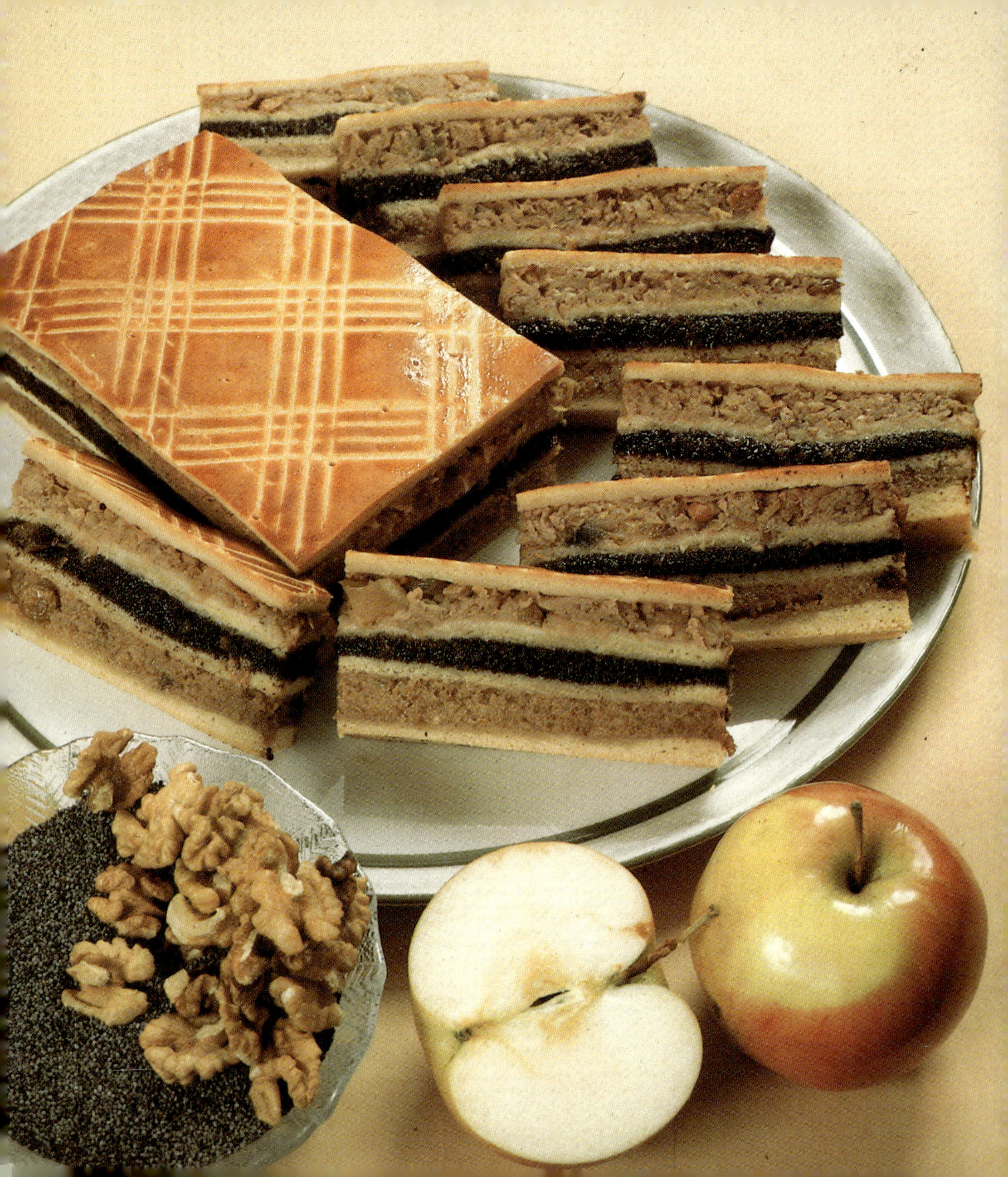

Milk Kolach

500 g (18 oz) plain flour, 2 eggs, 20 g (⅔ oz) yeast, 60–80 g (2–3 oz) butter, 225 ml (8 fl oz) milk, a pinch of salt, grated rind of 1 lemon, beaten egg for glazing

Heat the milk until lukewarm; mix with the sugar and yeast. Blend with the flour and eggs, add the salt and grated lemon rind, knead until the dough starts to form bubbles. Sprinkle the dough evenly with flour, cover with a towel and leave in a warm place to rise. Spread a thin layer of butter on top and roll together; place in a buttered baking tin and let it rise again. When the dough has risen, brush the uncovered dough with a beaten egg and bake in a moderate oven at 200 °C (400 °F, Gas Mark 6) for about 20 minutes.

Filled Kolach

Prepare a *yeast dough* using the ingredients and method described in the previous recipe.

For the filling: 60–80 g (2–3 oz) sugar, 100 g (4 oz) ground walnuts, 50 g (2 oz) raisins, 50–60 g (about 2 oz) butter, beaten egg for glazing

Roll out the risen dough and sprinkle a mixture of walnuts, sugar and soaked raisins on top. Spread evenly with the melted butter. Let it rest for a while, then paint the dough with beaten egg and bake in a buttered baking tin.

Kindli I
for Purim

For the dough: 1 kg (2 lb) plain flour, 250 g (9 oz) goose fat, 5 eggs, ½ glass of kosher (sweet red) wine
For the filling: 250 g (9 oz) walnuts, a handful of raisins, 4–5 tbs honey

Break the eggs into the flour, add the wine and knead until the dough becomes silky and smooth. Roll the dough into a very thin rectangle, spread with honey and sprinkle with warm goose fat, then sprinkle again with the walnuts, sugar, washed raisins, honey and goose fat. Roll up the

Flodni (Fluden)

dough and pierce the top with a fork. Brush with a mixture of the remaining goose fat and honey; bake. You may brush the kindli again towards the end of baking.

Poppy seeds may also be used for a filling. For this you will need 250 g (9 oz) poppy seeds, 3 tbs sugar, a little kosher (sweet red) wine mixed with water, a grated apple, and 4–5 tbs honey. Mix the ground poppy seeds, sugar, wine and water with the grated apple and honey, cook until thick. When cold, add the washed and soaked raisins. Fill the dough as described in the recipe above.

Kindli II

1 kg (2 lb) plain flour, 4 egg yolks, 300 g (11 oz) goose fat, 100 g (4 oz) icing sugar, a pinch of salt, 10 g (⅓ oz) yeast, water, 225 ml (8 fl oz) kosher (sweet red) wine, beaten egg for glazing
For the filling: 250 g (9 oz) ground walnuts, 3 tbs challah crumbs, 250 g (9 oz) sugar, grated rind of ½ lemon, a few tbs of kosher (sweet red) wine, 1 tbs lemon juice
For the poppy-seed filling: 250 g (9 oz) ground poppy seeds, 250 g (9 oz) sugar, 50 g (2 oz) raisins, grated rind of ½ lemon, 1 tsp lemon juice

Heat the milk until lukewarm and stir in the yeast. Blend with the fat, sugar, egg yolks, wine, salt, lemon juice and grated lemon rind. Let the dough rest, then divide into 8 pieces. Roll out each piece and fill the dough with the nut or poppy-seed filling. Turn up both edges and press down with your fingers, so that the pockets will be well sealed. Brush the top of the pastries with beaten egg so that they will have a nice golden, shiny finish. Bake until golden at 225 °C (435 °F, Gas Mark 7) for about 30 minutes.

Kindli III

500 g (18 oz) plain flour, 200 g (7 oz) goose fat, 3 egg yolks, 50 g (2 oz) sugar, a pinch of salt, 10 g (⅓ oz) yeast, grated rind of ½ lemon, ¼ tsp ground cloves, 2 tbs rum, beaten egg for glazing, and half the amounts of the ingredients used for the filling in the recipe above

Prepare the dough as in the recipe above, then divide it into four equal parts. Let it rest. Fill the dough, following the recipe above.

Flodni (Fluden)

500 g (18 oz) plain flour, 300 g (11 oz) butter or margarine, 4 eggs, 100 g (4 oz) sugar, 15 g (½ oz) yeast, 8 tbs kosher (sweet red) wine

The filling is the same as for the Kindli, but it is enriched with apples and jam

Prepare the dough as in the recipe above, let it rest, then divide it into 5 equal parts. Spread the prune jam (*lekvár*) on the bottom sheet, cover with a sheet of dough then spread it with the walnut mixture, cover with a third sheet of dough, spreading it in turn with poppy seeds, add another layer and top with grated apples (or apples stewed with cinnamon and sugar or honey), and then cover with the last sheet of dough. Brush the top sheet with a beaten egg so that the cake will have a nice golden finish. Bake slowly until golden at 200 °C (400 °F, Gas Mark 6) for about 40 minutes.

Hamantaschen
for Purim

250 g (9 oz) plain flour, 150 g (5 oz) margarine, 5 g (¼ oz) yeast, 4 tbs prune jam (lekvár) or 100 g (4 oz) poppy seeds, 100 g (4 oz) sugar, 2 eggs, grated rind of ½ lemon

Mix together the flour, sugar, eggs, melted margarine and lemon rind. Dissolve the yeast in a small amount of water and work into the flour mixture. Knead until a smooth dough is formed. Let it rest in a warm place for about 20–25 minutes. When the dough has doubled in size, roll it out and shape into a rectangle. Fill it with prune jam (*lekvár*) or poppy seeds, fold it in half, to form a pocket or a cap. Bake until golden at 200 °C (400 °F, Gas Mark 6) for about 30 minutes.

Kremlach I
for Passover

2 large potatoes, 3 eggs, ½ tsp salt, ground black pepper, oil

Peel and grate the potatoes and mix with the eggs, salt and pepper. Drop the batter by the spoonful into hot oil and fry on both sides.

Kremlach II
for Passover

5–6 tbs matzo meal, 6–7 eggs, 2 tbs goose fat, ½ tsp salt, ground black pepper, sugar, oil or goose fat for frying

Mix the egg yolks, goose fat, salt, pepper and matzo meal; gently fold in the stiffly beaten egg whites. Drop the batter by the spoonful into hot oil or goose fat and fry on both sides. *Optional:* sprinkle with sugar when serving.

Sweet Kremlach

3 eggs, 3 tsp lemon juice, a pinch of salt, 1–2 tsp grated lemon rind, 2 tbs matzo meal, 2 tbs sugar, oil for frying

Mix the eggs, salt, lemon juice, lemon rind, matzo meal and sugar. Blend until you get a thick batter that just drops from the spoon. Drop the batter by the spoonful into hot oil and fry on both sides.

Kremlach with Walnuts

3 eggs, 3 tbs sugar, 3 tsp lemon juice, 3 tbs ground walnuts, 3 tbs matzo meal

Mix together the egg yolks, sugar, ground walnuts, matzo meal and lemon juice. Gently fold in the stiffly beaten egg whites. Drop the batter by the spoonful into hot oil. Fry on both sides.

Matzo Meal Cake

7 tbs matzo meal, 7 tbs icing sugar, 7 eggs
For the filling: 250 g (9 oz) margarine, 3–4 tbs sugar, 1 egg yolk, 2 cubes of chocolate or 2 tsp cocoa, 1 tsp lemon juice

Beat the egg yolks and sugar until thick, sprinkle with matzo meal, then gently fold in the stiffly beaten egg whites. Line a baking tin with grease-proof paper, spoon the batter into the tin and bake very slowly at 180 °C (350 °F, Gas Mark 4) for about 50–60 minutes. Beat the margarine until creamy, then beat in the sugar and the egg yolks, add the softened chocolate (or cocoa) and the lemon rind.

When the cake cools, cut in two and fill with the lukewarm cream filling. Any leftover frosting may be spread on top and on the sides of the cake.

Matzo Brei

A few whole matzos, 1 glass kosher (sweet red) wine mixed with water
For the filling: 3 eggs, 3 tbs sugar, 2 tbs lemon juice, 3–4 tbs matzo meal,
oil for frying

Break the matzos in half, dip into the wine, then sandwich together two pieces of matzo with the filling and fry in hot oil on both sides.

Layered Matzo Cake

A few whole matzos, 1 glass kosher (sweet red) wine mixed with water
For the filling: 3 eggs, 3 tbs sugar, 3 tbs ground walnuts, 3 tbs matzo meal,
butter for greasing the tin

Break the matzos in half and dip them into the wine. Beat the egg yolks with the walnuts and matzo meal and fold in the stiffly beaten egg whites. Layer the matzos with the filling. Place the filled slices in a buttered tin and bake in a moderate oven at 200 °C (400 °F, Gas Mark 6) for about 30 minutes.

Matzo "French Toast"

4 eggs, juice and grated rind of ½ lemon, 2 tbs matzo meal, 2 whole
matzos, 1 glass kosher (sweet red) wine mixed with water, 4 tbs sugar,
a pinch of ground cinnamon, oil

Sprinkle the matzos with the wine and set them aside until they are soft. Cream the egg yolks with the sugar, add the lemon juice, grated lemon rind, matzo meal and work into a soft batter. Gently fold in the stiffly beaten egg whites. Spread this mixture on the matzos. Sprinkle cinnamon on each of the matzo squares. Fry the matzo "toasts" in hot oil. Serve dusted with a mixture of icing sugar and cinnamon.

Matzo with Apples

2 whole matzos, 1 glass of kosher (sweet red) wine mixed with water, 3 eggs, 3 tbs sugar, 50 g (2 oz) ground walnuts, 2 large apples, 1 stick of cinnamon, 1 tbs goose fat, a few drops of lemon juice

Sprinkle the matzos with wine and set them aside until they are soft. Slice the peeled apples, flavour them with cinnamon and lemon juice and simmer until soft. Beat the egg yolks and sugar until creamy; gently fold in the stiffly beaten egg whites. Place a matzo in a well-greased baking tin, spread with the apple filling, top with another matzo and cover with the egg mixture. Keep alternating the fillings. Spread the top layer with goose fat and bake slowly.

Kreplach Filled with Cottage or Curd Cheese
for Shavuot

350 g (13 oz) plain flour, 2 eggs, pinch of salt
For the filling: 500 g (18 oz) cottage cheese, icing sugar, 4–5 tbs challah crumbs

Knead the flour, eggs, salt and sufficient water to make a smooth non-sticky dough. Roll out on a floured board until transparent and as thin as a knife blade. Dot with a teaspoonful of filling at regular intervals, fold and cover the filled pieces with dough. Press the edges firmly to seal. Cut with a ravioli cutter into bite-sized pieces and drop them into boiling salted water. Lift out with a perforated spoon and put them into a colander to drain. Sprinkle with browned challah crumbs and icing sugar.

Apple Slices

500 g (18 oz) plain flour, 200 g (7 oz) margarine, 1–2 eggs, juice and grated rind of ½ lemon, 3–5 tbs sour cream, 6–7 large apples, 60–70 g (2–2½ oz) ground walnuts, 200 g (7 oz) sugar, a pinch of ground cinnamon, a pinch of salt, beaten egg for glazing

Mix the flour, eggs, margarine, sour cream, sugar and salt gently into a dough. Grate the peeled apples and mix with the sugar and cinnamon. Roll out half the pastry to fit a shallow tin. Sprinkle with the walnuts, then cover with the grated apples. Roll out the remaining pastry and cover the filling. Pierce the top with a fork in a few places and brush with beaten egg to give the apple slices a nice shiny surface when baked.

Plum Dumplings

500 g (18 oz) potatoes, 1 egg, 2–3 tbs melted margarine or butter, plain flour as needed, a pinch of salt, 500 g (18 oz) plums, 5 tbs challah crumbs

Rice the boiled an peeled potatoes. Mix with the eggs, salt, melted margarine and flour to give a soft, easily handled dough. If the dough becomes too soft, add more flour. Roll out on a floured board and cut into rectangles. Place a washed and pitted plum in the middle of each rectangle. Wet your hands and form small balls from the dough. Drop the filled dumplings into boiling water, cook, drain and roll in the browned challah crumbs.

Cabbage Strudel

Strudel pastry sheet.
For the filling: 1 small head of cabbage, salt, ground black pepper, 6–7 tbs oil, some sugar, challah crumbs

Wash and shred the cabbage using a cabbage shredder, salt and leave for a while. Drain and dry thoroughly. Brown in a small amount of oil until golden.
Sprinkle the strudel sheet with oil and challah crumbs. Mix the cooled cabbage with sugar and pepper to taste, arrange the filling on the strudel sheet, then carefully roll it up like a Swiss roll. Brush the top with oil and bake at 190 °C (375 °F, Gas Mark 5) for about 30–35 minutes.

Potato Strudel

Strudel pastry sheet.
For the filling: 4 large potatoes, 4 eggs, 4 tbs sugar, grated rind of 1 lemon, 50 g (2 oz) ground almonds

Brush the strudel sheet with oil or goose fat. To prepare the filling: Boil the potatoes, and peel them whilst they are still warm. Rice the potatoes and add the egg yolks together with the stiffly beaten egg whites, sugar, and lemon rind. Blend well and then add the ground walnuts. Spread the filling on the strudel sheet, roll up like a Swiss roll, turn in the edges and bake slowly as in the above recipe.

Cake for Passover

4 eggs, 2 tbs sugar, 4 tbs grated potatoes, a pinch of salt, fat for greasing

Blend the grated raw potatoes with the egg yolks, salt and sugar. Fold in the stiffly beaten egg whites and pour into a well-greased dish or cake tin. Bake at 180 °C (350 °F, Gas Mark 4) for about 20 minutes. When cool, cut the cake into squares and serve.

Spice Cake

250 g (9 oz) butter, 250 g (9 oz) sugar, 2 cubes of chocolate, 1 tsp ground cinnamon, a pinch of ground cloves, vanilla sugar, grated rind of ½ lemon, 100–150 g (4–5 oz) potato flour, 250 g (9 oz) semolina

Beat the eggs with the sugar until foamy. Add the potato flour and semolina, blend in the melted margarine and the softened chocolate. Gently fold in the stiffly beaten egg whites. Butter a cake tin, pour in the batter, cover with grease-proof paper and bake slowly at 180 °C (350 °F, Gas Mark 4) for about 50 minutes.

Layered Matzo Cake

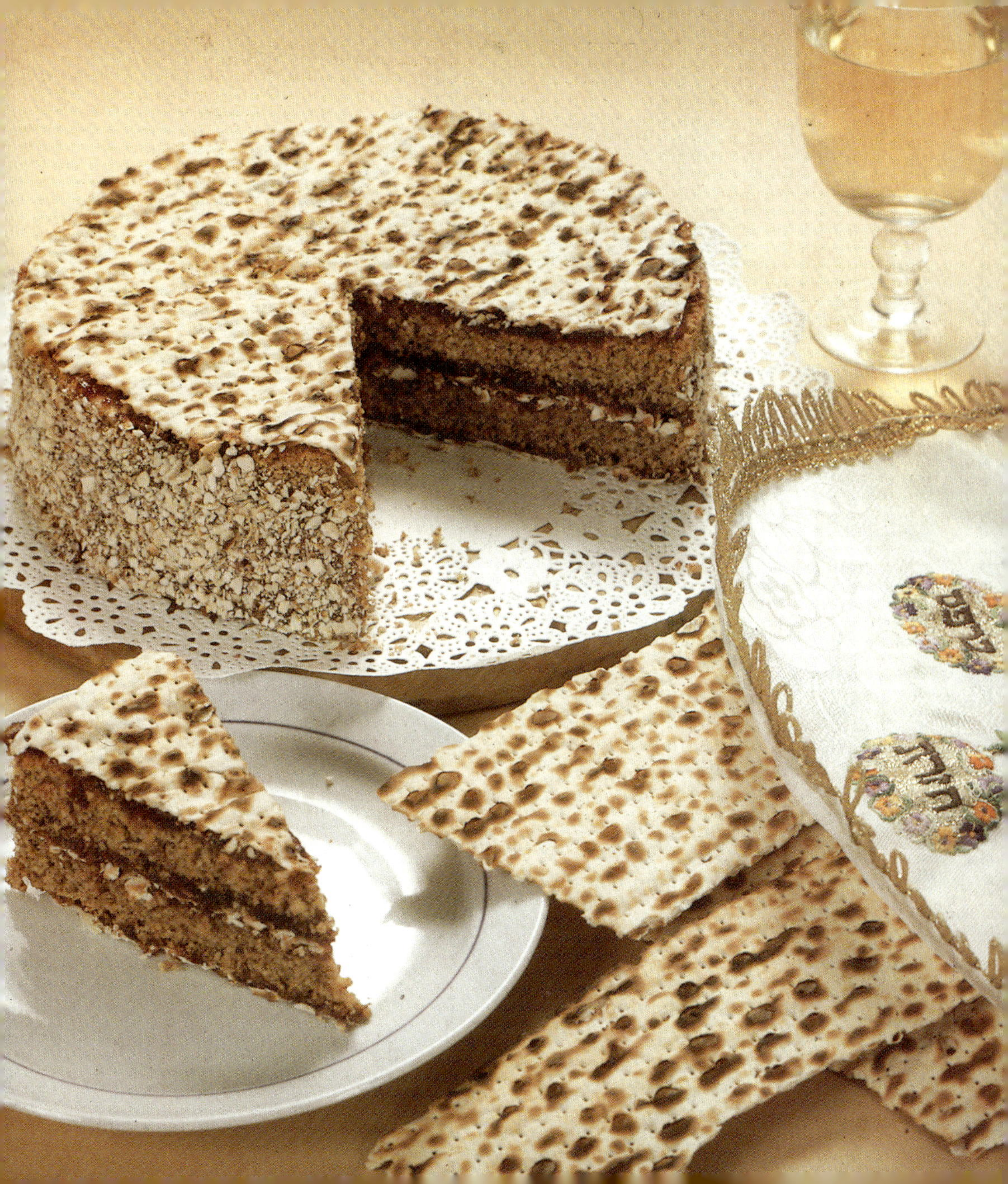

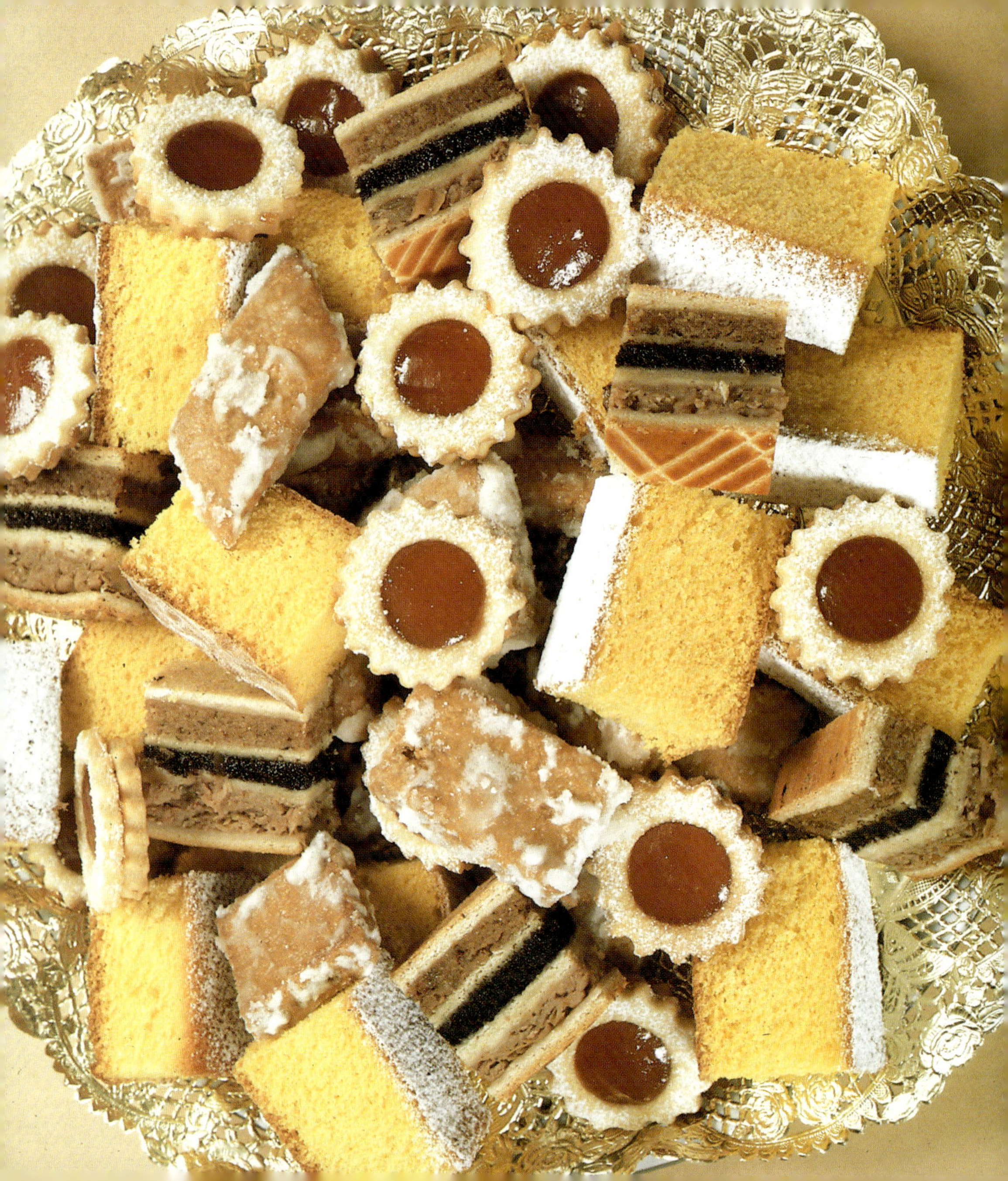

TABLE OF RECIPES

Almond Soup 29
Apple Kugel 59
Apple Sauce 33
Apple Slices 70

Barley with Fried Onion 35
Barley Soup I 27
Barley Soup II 28
Beef Soup 24
Beetroot Borscht 27
Beetroot Borscht for Passover 27
Bouillon 25
Braised Beef 48
Braised Brisket 47

Cabbage with Beans 35
Cabbage Strudel 71
Cake for Passover 72
Carrots 38
Chestnut Sauce 34
Chicken Soup 24
Cholent I 39
Cholent II 39
Cholent III 40
Cinnamon Apples 38
Cooked Potato Kugel I 31
Cooked Potato Kugel II 32
Cucumber Sauce with Raisins 33

Dairy Tomato Soup 27
Dumplings (Spaetzli) 32

Egg and Onion Spread I 57
Egg and Onion Spread II 57
Eierkuchen I 61
Eierkuchen II 61
Eierkuchen III 61

Farvli with Stuffed Neck 36
Feferkuchen Spice Cake 60
Filled Kolach 65
Fish Polonaise 44
Fish Soup with Sour Cream and Egg Yolks 28
Fish with Walnuts I 43
Fish with Walnuts II 43
Fish with Walnuts III 44
Fishroe Soup 28
Flodni 67
Fried Goose Liver 52
Fried Goose or Duck Liver 53

Galantine of Goose I 51
Galantine of Goose II 52
Garlic Soup I 26
Garlic Soup II 26
Gefillte Helzel I 45
Gefillte Helzel II 46
Gingerbread I 60
Gingerbread II 60
Golden Vegetable Pot Roast 47
Goldzip—Golden Soup 25
Goose Sausage with Lungs 51
Goulash Soup 25
Green Beans 38

Mixed Cake Platter

Hamantaschen 67
Horse-radish Sauce with Raisins 34

Inarsz 57

Jellied Fish I 42
Jellied Fish II 42
Jellied Pike 42

Kindli I 65
Kindli II 66
Kindli III 66
Knaidlach (Matzo Balls) I 31
Knaidlach (Matzo Balls) II 31
Kranzli 63
Kremlach I 67
Kremlach II 68
Kremlach with Walnuts 68
Kreplach 30
Kreplach Filled with Cottage or Curd Cheese 70
Krotzip (Cabbage Soup) I 26
Krotzip (Cabbage Soup) II 26
Kugel 61
Kugel I 40
Kugel II 40
Kugel III 40
Kugel IV 41
Kugel V 41
Kugel VI 41

Layered Matzo Cake 69
Layered Potatoes 37
Lekach (Honey and Spice Cake) 62
Liver Dumplings 53
Liver Sausage 56
Lokshen Kugel I 59
Lokshen Kugel II 59

Lung Kreplach 30
Lung Sausage I 55
Lung Sausage II 55
Lung with Garlic 54

Matzo Brei 69
Matzo "French Toast" 69
Matzo Meal Cake 68
Matzo with Apples 70
Meat Kugel 49
Milk Kolach 65
Millet 35
Mish-mash Delkli 64
Mock Calf's-Head Cheese 57
Mock Fish I 48
Mock Fish II 49

Ox-Tongue in Raisin Sauce 47

Passover Cake 72
Pcha (Calf's-foot Jelly) 56
Peppers Stuffed with Pike 41
Pike Stuffed with Walnuts 43
Pike with Sour Cream 44
Plum Dumplings 71
Potato Cake 62
Potato Kugel 36
Potato Strudel 71
Prunes with Rice 35

Raisin Sauce 33
Roast Leg of Goose I 52
Roast Leg of Goose II 52

Schmaltzbaigli 63
Serbian Fish 45
Sour-cherry Sauce 34
Spice Cake 72

Split Peas 37
Stuffed Breast of Goose 50
Stuffed Cabbage 39
Stuffed Casings 53
Stuffed Goose Neck 51
Stuffed Pike I 46
Stuffed Pike II 46
Stuffed Turkey Neck I 49
Stuffed Turkey Neck II 50
Stuffed Turkey Neck III 50
Sweet-and-Sour Fish 45
Sweet Kremlach 68

Teiglach (Honey Buckles) 62
Tsimmes 36

Veal Krezli 56

Weisskinlach (Wine Biscuits) I 64
Weisskinlach (Wine Biscuits) II 64

Zatterka 63

Printed in Hungary, 1989
Kner Printing House, Békéscsaba
CO 2693–h–8890

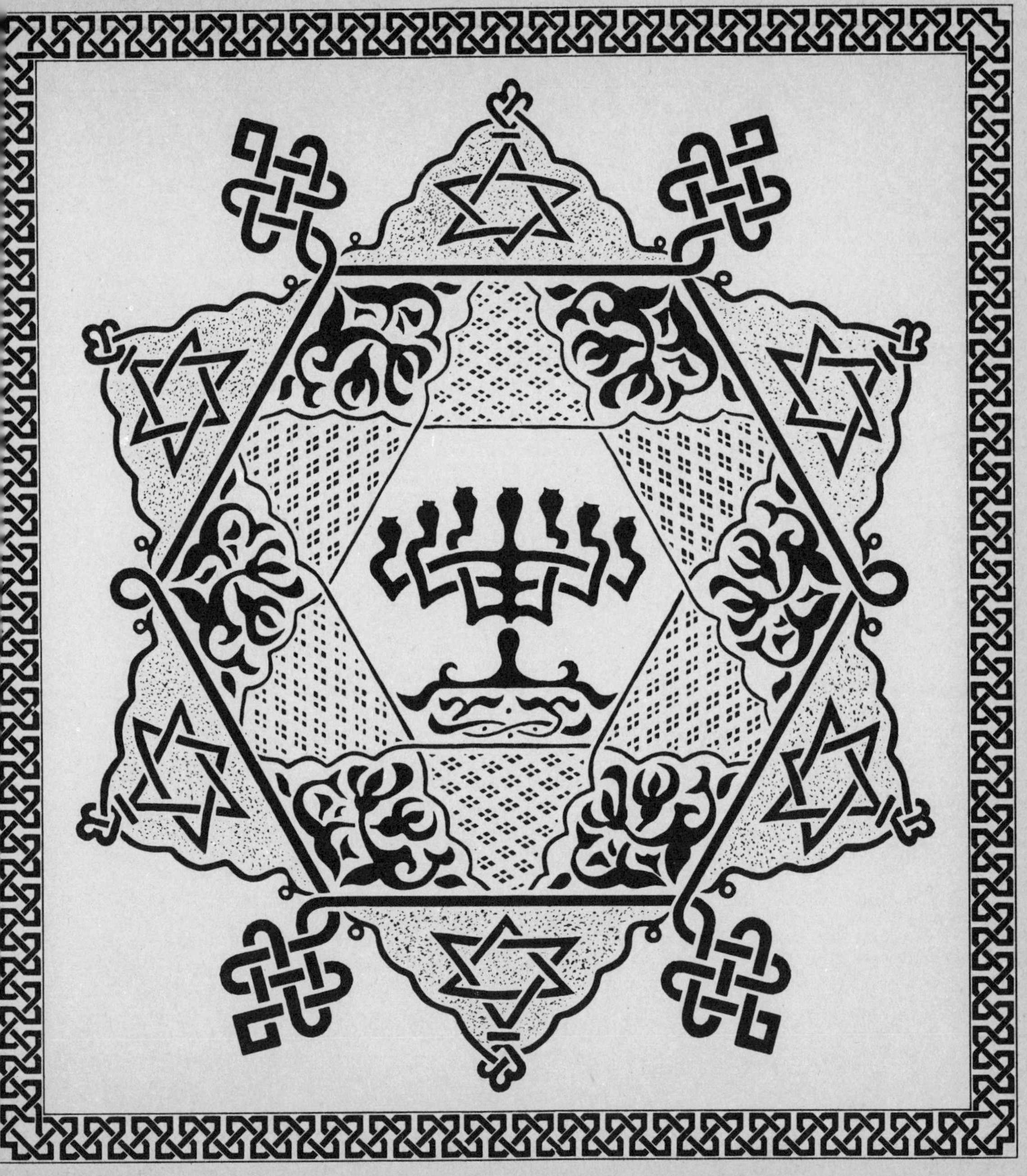

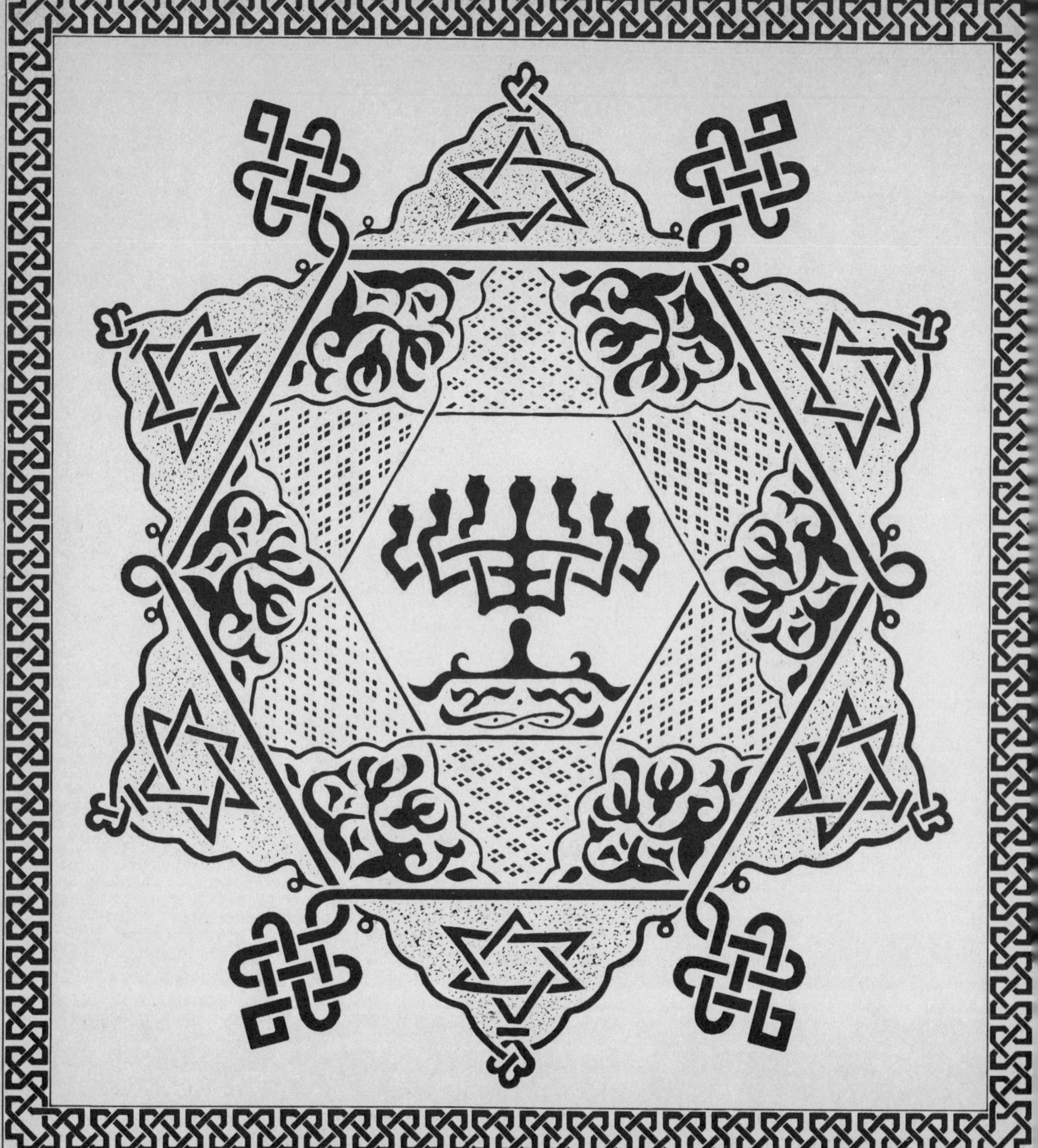

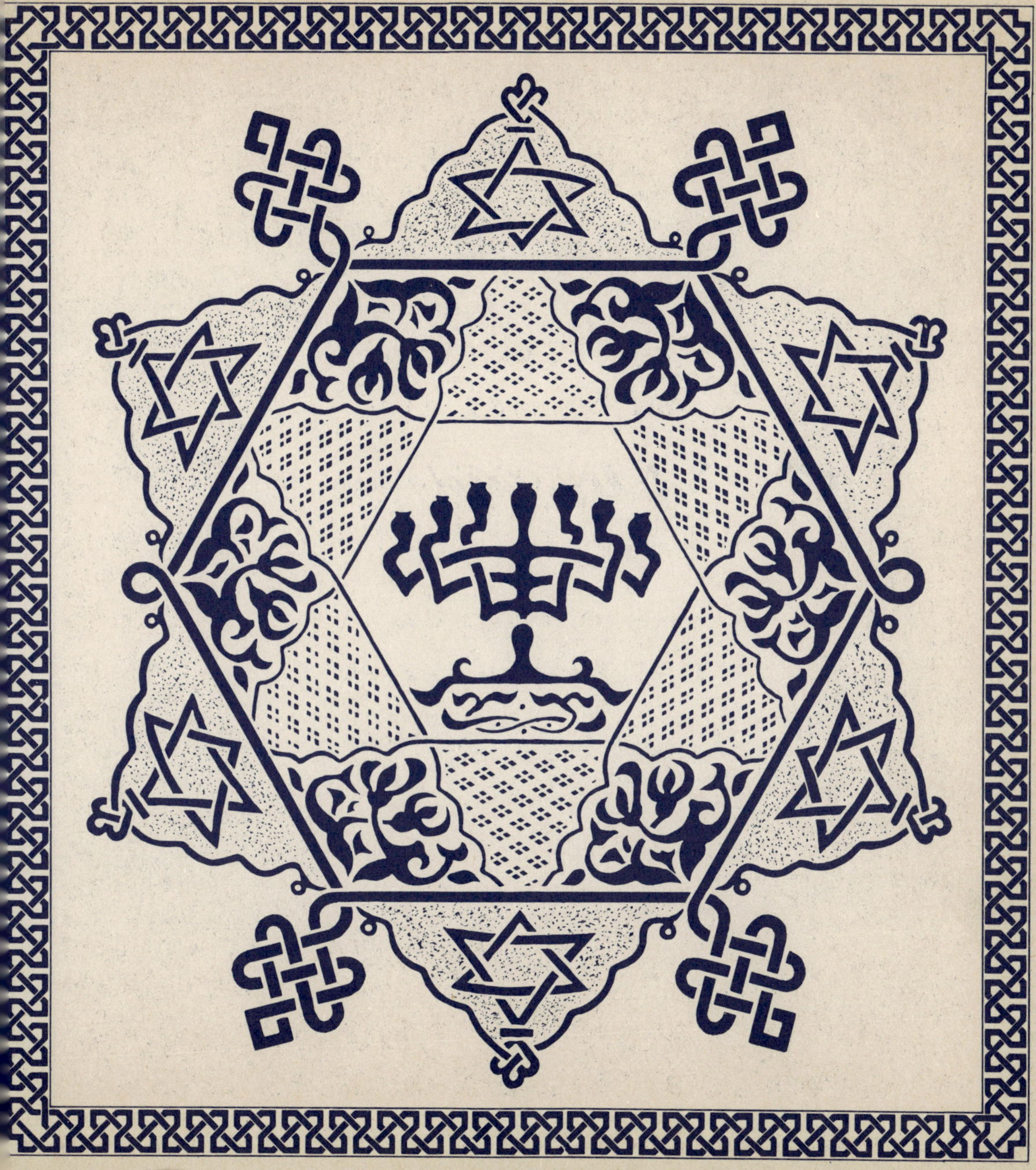

מאכלים מסורתיים במשפחה היהודית